Overcoming Fear and Panic Attacks

A Guide to Understanding, Managing, and Thriving Beyond Anxiety and Panic

Dr. Mashal Al Nawab

MBChB, DipRCPath, CCST, FRCPath, PhD (London)

Copyright © 2023 Dr. Mashal Al Nawab

All rights reserved.

ISBN: 9798863886671

To My Family

CONTENTS

Preface

1	Understanding Panic Attacks	1
2	Identifying and Categorising Panic Attacks – Diagnosis and Assessment	34
3	Managing and Treating Panic Attacks – *A Mindset Modification Approach*	49
4	Thriving Beyond Panic Attacks	112
5	Looking Towards the Future	132
6	About the Author	146

PREFACE

A growing number of us are realising that anxiety and panic are unpleasant companions that coexist within the context of our fast-moving and demanding lifestyles. As the pace of life seems to accelerate with each passing day, these unseen foes may seize control of our minds and bodies, making us feel powerless and entrapped.

Age, gender, ethnicity, and socioeconomic class are all irrelevant when it comes to experiencing anxiety and panic attacks. They are widespread and at times all-consuming. However, the important facts are that neither our anxieties nor panic attacks define who we are.

I am both a medically qualified, and a Ph.D., doctor, but I do not purport to write this book as a trained psychiatrist or psychologist, of which I am neither. I do so as a highly qualified medical professional who, in the past, has suffered from panic attacks related to a post-traumatic stress disorder (PTSD). As such, I am very familiar with the subject matter, have been in your shoes, and I am able to view the subject from both ends of a spectrum.

As a dyslexic, I am well aware that, I am more prone to panic disorder than others. I experienced PTSD in my early twenties as the result of a particular sequence of unfortunate life events. At that time, the diagnosis of PTSD was not sufficiently recognised or understood as it is today.

The feature or symptom that distressed me the most in the condition was the accompanying panic disorder with its unpredictably occurring panic episodes. It took considerable in-depth self-analysis as well as research to finally understand the condition and get a firm handle on it.

The purpose of this book is to provide you, the Reader, with an enhanced understanding of panic attacks and anxiety, their causes, and their main features. Additionally, it should embed within you a mindset that enables you to reclaim the authority and self-control that panic may have stripped away from you.

In this book you will find a tremendous weapon that will help you change the way you relate to anxiety and panic attacks and ultimately dominate them.

The Reader should keep in mind that the road to recovery is not a straight one. Ups and downs, twists, and turns will be part of the journey. However, you will find your way to a life free of anxiety and panic if you achieve the mindset change and concept lock-in presented here.

Know that when it comes to defeating anxiety and panic, knowledge is truly king.

CHAPTER 1

UNDERSTANDING PANIC ATTACKS

Introduction

Many have quoted Lao Tzu as saying that "if you are depressed you are living in the past. If you are anxious you are living in the future. But if you are at peace, you are living in the present moment". Many of my age group will recall the slogan "live in the Now" as a cry resonating throughout the baby boomer generation. Nowadays, it seems that many in our modern societies are psychologically either living in the past or in the future but not in the present.

The frequency and complexity of panic attacks and the associated sense of anxiety have a pronounced negative influence on a person's quality of life. These two related phenomena frequently cross paths but also have unique traits and motivations.

Panic attacks are intense and sudden surges of extreme fear or dread, that can seemingly arise out of nowhere. They are characterised by a range of distressing physical and psychological symptoms, such as rapid heartbeat, shortness of breath, trembling, and a pervasive sense of impending doom. Anxiety, on the other hand, is a broader and more persistent emotional state typified by excessive worry, fear, and apprehension about future events or situations. While anxiety often manifests in a milder and more sustained form, it can also sometimes escalate into panic attacks.

This book is written for those who suffer from these

phenomena or for those who want help family or friends manage these challenging emotional states, and where gaining a firm understanding of panic and anxiety is essential.

The text will also underscore a proper concept lock-in and mindset-modifying approach for the control and elimination of panic attacks. It will also be citing supplementary treatment methods that can help more rapidly accomplish and lock-in that therapeutic method.

It will further delve into the definitions, causes, symptoms, and potential treatments for panic attacks and anxiety. It will discuss the role that genetics and environmental factors may play in the development of these conditions, as well as the neurological and physiological mechanisms that underlie these experiences. Moreover, it will explore various therapeutic strategies, medications, and complementary approaches, that can aid in managing and alleviating the symptoms of panic attacks and anxiety. Ultimately, it is the central theme of better understanding coupled with a mindset change that will empower individuals to effectively address and navigate the challenges posed by panic attacks and anxiety.

For those who want to quickly know how to tackle the issue of panic then the fundamental treatment application in this book can be found in chapter 3. Nevertheless, keep in mind that the first two chapters will lay down important groundwork for a firmer understanding of the aliment itself.

What are Panic Attacks

Panic attacks are episodes of acute apprehension or anxiety that come on suddenly and fiercely and last for only a few minutes. These episodes frequently happen without any obvious cause or warning and can be overpowering and

Overcoming Fear and Panic Attacks

incapacitating. The symptoms of a panic attack include Shortness of breath, tightness in the throat and/or difficulty swallowing, accelerated heartbeat (palpitations) and discomfort in the chest. There will be a sense of impending doom or dread of losing control accompanied by trembling, or shaking, excessive sweating, dizziness or light-headedness, nausea or stomach pain, numbness or tingling sensation, hot flashes, or chills. These symptoms may manifest individually or in different combinations. Very frequently, people who suffer panic attacks for the first time, fear for their lives thinking that their systems are failing or that they are losing control of their minds.

While panic attacks are sometimes experienced as singular incidents, some people may experience recurrent attacks and develop what is known as panic disorder. This is characterised by frequent, unexpected panic attacks as well as a constant worry about experiencing further attacks (i.e., they develop a "fear of fear cycle").

Therapies such as cognitive-behavioural therapy and, in some situations, medication help and support in controlling symptoms and lessening the frequency and severity of panic attacks. They are among the more common treatment options used to address panic disorder and isolated panic episodes.
This book will show you how to make a clear mindset shift in order to address panic as part of an overall treatment.

Recognising Panic Disorder in Contrast to Other Anxiety Disorders

It is important to consider the distinctive traits, signs, and diagnostic standards connected with each anxiety syndrome while separating panic disorder from other anxiety-associated conditions. To assist in distinguishing panic disorder from other prevalent anxiety disorders, the following are some crucial points:

Recurring and sudden panic attacks are the main symptoms of panic disorder. In those with panic disorder, panic attacks are frequently short, lasting only several minutes. The panic episodes themselves are the main emphasis since they are frequently viewed by the sufferer as very serious or life-threatening. As a result of dread from having panic attacks in front of others or in crowded locations, some people with panic disorder may develop agoraphobia, which entails avoiding circumstances or places where they anticipate a panic attack could happen. Agoraphobia is an anxiety disorder distinguished by a pronounced and severe dread about being in circumstances or locations where escaping would be challenging, or aid might not be easily accessible when a person suffers the distressing symptoms of panic attacks.

Generalised Anxiety Disorder (GAD)

Central Features

GAD is typified by excessive and uncontrolled concern and anxiety about many different elements of life. People suffering GAD display long-term, excessive worry and anxiety that is well beyond what is normal or appropriate for regular everyday concerns. This excessive worry can make it difficult to function day to day and can cause major suffering. GAD salient characteristics include:

Disproportionate Distress

People with GAD worry excessively about a variety of things, including their health, their jobs, their money, their relationships, and many other things. The worry is frequently

Overcoming Fear and Panic Attacks

unfounded but hard to manage.

Physical Symptoms

GAD can also present with physical symptoms such as muscular tension, restlessness, exhaustion, irritability, trouble focusing, and sleep difficulties, in addition to the psychological manifestations.

Relaxation Challenges

People with GAD frequently have trouble relaxing and may be anxious, perplexed and tense all the time.

Impact on Performance

The excessive worry and physical symptoms of GAD can seriously disrupt everyday functioning, making it challenging to focus, perform at work or school, maintain relationships, and participate in social activities.

GAD frequently coexists with other anxiety disorders, such as depression, and other mental health issues. However, it is the incessant worry that is the focus here, rather than frequent panic attacks. While people with GAD may worry and feel anxious about a variety of things, they usually do not have frequent, unexpected panic episodes. Psychologists and psychiatrists are frequently involved in the diagnosis and treatment of GAD.
The various treatment modalities include:

Psychotherapy

Cognitive-behavioural therapy (CBT)
CBT is a popular and successful type of therapy for GAD. CBT aids in the identification of harmful thinking patterns, their modification, and the development of coping

mechanisms for anxiety management.

Medication

In some circumstances, doctors may recommend medication, such as benzodiazepines or selective serotonin reuptake inhibitors (SSRIs), to alleviate moderate GAD symptoms.

Lifestyle Modifications

Changing to a healthy lifestyle that includes regular exercise, a balanced diet, sleep promotion and stress-reduction strategies can help to control GAD symptoms. GAD is a curable condition, and many sufferers may significantly improve their quality of life with the appropriate mix of counselling and medication. To effectively manage GAD, early intervention and continued assistance are essential.

Depression and Panic Attacks

Depression is one of the most prevalent mental health conditions globally. It is characterised by persistent feelings of melancholy, despair, and a lack of interest in daily activities. On the other hand, panic attacks are abrupt, severe bouts of terror or high anxiety that are frequently accompanied by physical symptoms like shortness of breath and a racing heart. Despite having a seemingly separate nature, these conditions have a complex interaction that can profoundly affect a person's general well-being.
This complicated connection between depression and panic attacks can represent a very difficult experience indeed for individuals afflicted.

The Confluence of Panic Attacks and Depression

Overcoming Fear and Panic Attacks

It is not unusual for people to have panic attacks and depression at the same time. According to studies, those who are depressed are more prone to experience panic attacks or acquire a panic disorder; the opposite is also true. As mentioned, the diagnosis and treatment processes may become more challenging when these disorders coexist.

Imbalance in neurotransmitters like serotonin and noradrenaline are thought to be major causes of both depression and panic episodes. Increased stress reactions, anxiety, and mood changes can all be caused by the dysregulation of these brain chemicals. The symptoms of panic attacks and depression frequently coincide. For instance, both conditions may have symptoms including weariness, restlessness, irritability, and sleep difficulties. It can be tough to distinguish between them because of this overlap, making it challenging to differentiate between the two.
Depression and panic episodes when they go hand in hand, create a vicious cycle. Anxiety levels might rise because of depressive symptoms, which can then result in panic attacks. On the other hand, the accompanying dread and anguish of panic attacks can make depression symptoms worse.

Effect on Patients

When depression and panic episodes coexist, they frequently manifest as more severe and resistant to therapy. A serious impairment in everyday functioning may result from their cumulative effects on mental health. Due to the dread of having panic attacks, people may withdraw from social situations, their jobs, or their schooling, leading them to isolate themselves and experience even more depression-related symptoms. Some people who are coping with the difficulties of depression and panic attacks may resort to drugs or alcohol as a method to self-medicate and numb their emotional suffering. This raises the risk of developing substance abuse disorders.

Management and Treatment

The Complete Approach

It is frequently necessary to take a wide-ranging and comprehensive approach to treating depression and panic attacks. This usually involves medication (such as antidepressants or anti-anxiety drugs), psychotherapy (such as cognitive-behavioural therapy), and lifestyle modifications (such as regular exercise and stress management).

Addressing Underlying Causes

It is critical to recognise and address the underlying causes of both conditions. Investigating prior trauma, unresolved sorrow, or persistent stresses will be necessary to achieve this.

Building a solid support network that consists of family, friends, as well as, and mental health specialists is essential for those who are coping with both conditions. During trying circumstances, such support may offer both practical help and emotional understanding. (further see Support Network Chapter 5).

The connection between panic episodes and depression is complex and nuanced. These disorders can feed off each other, increasing misery and limiting everyday functioning. However, people may overcome these problems with the appropriate care, encouragement, and coping mechanisms. An individual's well-being and quality of life can be greatly enhanced by early intervention as well as a holistic approach to treating both depression and panic attacks. To break the cycle of despair and anxiety and eventually promote hope and resilience, it is crucial to understand how these symptoms are interrelated and to seek treatment when

Overcoming Fear and Panic Attacks

necessary.

Social Phobia (Social Anxiety Disorder)

Defined as extreme anxiety or fear of social and performance situations. A severe and enduring dread of social and performance settings where one could be watched, and scrutinised by others is the defining feature of this mental health problem. People with social anxiety disorder frequently worry excessively about being humiliated, shamed, or poorly judged by others.

Social Anxiety Disorder's Key Characteristics

The fear of social settings is the main characteristic of social anxiety disorder. Public speaking, attending gatherings, making calls, mingling with strangers, and taking part in group activities are a few examples of these circumstances.

People who struggle with social anxiety may go to considerable measures to stay away from circumstances that make them feel anxious. They could turn down social invitations, miss classes or meetings, or refrain from speaking in front of others.

Physical signs of social anxiety include flushing, sweating, shaking, a quick heartbeat, nausea, and a sense of being lightheaded or dizzy. People who suffer from social anxiety disorder frequently have unfavourable self-assessments and may worry excessively about what other people think of them. They can be concerned that they may say or do anything unpleasant or embarrassing.

An individual's capacity to function at work or school, maintain relationships, and engage in daily activities can all be negatively impacted by social anxiety. If left untreated, social anxiety disorder can become chronic and often lasts

months or more, thus impacting quality of life.
In contrast to simple shyness, it is a diagnosable mental condition that will need to be treated.

Social Anxiety Disorder Treatment

For social anxiety, cognitive behaviour therapy is a popular and successful treatment option. It supports people in recognising and challenging harmful thought patterns, creating coping mechanisms, and progressively facing their fears in various social circumstances.

To assist in the control of symptoms, doctors may occasionally prescribe drugs like anti-anxiety drugs or selective serotonin reuptake inhibitors (SSRIs). To gradually lessen anxiety, some therapists also use Exposure Therapy. Patients on whom exposure therapy is used are progressively exposed to social situations they dread but in a safe and supportive setting.

Support groups also have a useful role to play in patient management. In these support groups, social anxiety sufferers can practise social skills and receive support from others who have gone through similar situations.

Whereas socially anxious people feel anxious and exhibit physical symptoms only while in certain social circumstances. They do not, as a rule, have frequent, unplanned panic episodes unrelated to that particular social context.

With the correct mix of counselling, medicine, and family support, many people with social anxiety disorder significantly improve their quality of life. Social anxiety disorder is a curable condition, but for management to be most effective, early intervention is important.

Overcoming Fear and Panic Attacks

Specific Phobias

The principal characteristics for specific phobias include severe fear and avoidance of very particular triggers (e.g., fear of snakes, dogs, spiders etc.). Panic episodes are not usually a characteristic; instead, the focus is on the phobic trigger. When faced with their fear, people with specific phobias will feel anxious and exhibit panic-like symptoms but they are quite comfortable in circumstances not related to their triggers.

Obsessive-Compulsive Disorder (OCD)

Obsessions (intrusive, upsetting thoughts) and/or compulsions (repetitive behaviour or mental acts) are the main characteristics of this condition. Obsessive-Compulsive Disorder (OCD) is a mental health disorder depicted by obsessions and/or compulsions that seriously disrupt a person's functioning and cause them marked discomfort. Because the obsessions and compulsions are frequently motivated by worry or the wish to lessen anxiety, it is classified as an anxiety disorder.

Crucial elements of OCD include:

Uncontrollably invasive, disturbing, and repeating thoughts, desires, or mental pictures are known as obsessions. These ideas frequently generate severe worry or discomfort and are illogical. Frequent obsessions include intrusive thoughts about religion or sexuality, ideas of harming oneself or others, a need for symmetry or order, and worries of contamination.

On the other hand, compulsions are habitual actions or thoughts that a person feels driven to carry out because of their obsession. These actions are meant to lessen the worry or discomfort that the obsessions are causing. Repeated hand washing, checking locks, counting, organising items in a certain manner, and looking to other people for comfort are examples of common compulsions.

It should be kept in mind that all of us exhibit a certain degree of OCD behaviours. An example: anyone who wears or carries a certain item of clothing repetitively when taking exams because they are "lucky" are exhibiting an OCD mannerism. It is only when these obsessions and compulsions become extremely distressing, consume a significant amount of time (typically more than an hour per day), and interfere with a person's ability to go about their everyday lives that they are diagnosed as suffering from OCD.

While some OCD sufferers believe their thoughts and behaviours are entirely reasonable or even true, (referred to as absent insight/delusional beliefs), others may be convinced that their obsessions and compulsions are reasonable but not true, (referred to as poor insight), while still others see them as unreasonable and irrational and untrue (referred to as good or fair insight). The degree of OCD varies; some people have moderate symptoms, while others have more severe cases that can be quite incapacitating. Despite being seen as a chronic condition, it is nevertheless quite curable.

The standard course of treatment for OCD includes a mix of treatments, such as:

CBT, the topic of Cognitive-Behavioural Therapy is reviewed in Chapter 3. One kind of CBT that works quite well for OCD is exposure and response prevention, or ERP. ERP entails exposing the sufferer to frightening circumstances or ideas gradually and under controlled conditions, and without allowing them to revert back to

Overcoming Fear and Panic Attacks

obsessive habits.

Medications

Prescription drugs like selective serotonin reuptake inhibitors (SSRIs) are frequently given to treat OCD symptoms.

Support Groups

Group therapy or support groups can offer a helpful setting for people with OCD to discuss their experiences and coping mechanisms.

The focus is on compulsions and obsessions, with the aim of reducing the distress resulting from obsessions. It is anxiety, not panic attacks, that is the primary symptom related to OCD.

Effective OCD management and enhancing the quality of life for those afflicted with the illness depend on early diagnosis and therapy. Although OCD can be a difficult disorder to manage, many people can significantly reduce their symptoms and enhance their functioning abilities with the right help.

It is crucial to remember that people might have co-morbid diagnoses, which means they could be dealing with many anxiety disorders at once.
A comprehensive assessment by a mental health specialist is necessary for a precise diagnosis and for setting a suitable treatment strategy. Since differential diagnosis can be complicated, a thorough evaluation is necessary to ascertain the best course of action for treating anxiety-related issues.

Typical Signs and Triggers of Anxiety and Panic

Although anxiety is a natural and adaptive reaction to stress or perceived dangers, it can be categorised as an anxiety disorder when it becomes excessive, persistent, or interferes with day-to-day functioning.

Anxiety's typical signs and symptoms include:

Generalised Nervousness

Excessive and ongoing concern over several facets of life, often coupled with a sense of approaching disaster or doom. This frequently coexists with restlessness, difficulty unwinding, and susceptibility to be easily startled.

Physical Signals

Anxiety frequently shows up physically, causing symptoms like: Heart palpitations (fast heartbeat), tension and pains in the muscles, dysphagia or difficulty in swallowing, breathlessness when speaking with difficulty in enunciation, mild shaking or trembling, increased perspiration and sweating not related to effort or heat, nausea or upset stomach, feeling lightheaded or dizzy, blurring of vision, experiencing ongoing tiredness or mental exhaustion because of heightened awareness of one's surroundings.

The patients are often unusually short tempered or become rapidly agitated. There is a challenge focusing on reading a book or article, making decisions, or recalling details. There is frequently a disturbance in sleep and insomnia or poor sleep habits. This may manifest as behavioural changes such as keeping the light on when sleeping when previously they preferred darkness, or sleeping in the same room with someone or something that makes them feel safe. As you seem to take your anxiety with you wherever you go, it

Overcoming Fear and Panic Attacks

becomes difficult to escape or get respite from it. Therefore, it needs to be addressed head on.

Typical Triggers

Stressful Life Events or significant life transitions, including relocating, changing careers, or going through a breakup, can set off anxiety attacks. Also, pressure from work or school where anxiety might be brought on by heavy workloads, deadlines, tests, or performance reviews.

Health Concerns where being concerned about one's own health or the health of those close to one. Social Situations that promote social anxiety disorder. These can be social gatherings, speeches in front of an audience, or meeting new people. Also, anxiety can arise from worries around finances, debt, or job security. Trauma where anxiety may be a result of past traumatic events including abuse, assault, or accidents.

Biology and Genetics may play a role; anxiety disorders may have a hereditary component for certain people, and abnormalities in brain chemistry may also be involved.
Substance abuse with use of stimulants, alcohol, or coffee among other substances, can intensify or cause anxiety symptoms.

A crucial point to remember, not everyone experiences anxiety in the same way, and not everyone will have the same symptoms or causes. Furthermore, although anxiety is a natural part of life, severe and persistent anxiety that substantially impairs day-to-day functioning calls for professional assessment and treatment, which may include counselling and, in certain situations, medication.

The Science Behind Panic

Complex interactions between the brain, nervous system, and other physiological and psychological components are at play in the initiation of panic. Understanding the science of panic in panic disorder is of great importance.

Structure and Function of the Brain

An important factor in panic is the amygdala, a region of the brain involved in processing emotions and the perception of danger. Perceiving danger can set off the body's "fight or flight" reaction, even in situations where the risk is not immediate or immediately tangible. An hyperresponsive or hyperactive amygdala may be a factor in the development of panic episodes.

Chemical Messengers

The brain's chemical messengers, including noradrenaline and serotonin, are important in controlling anxiety and mood. Panic disorder and other anxiety disorders are linked to imbalances in these neurotransmitters. In treating panic disorder medication is often used to correct any imbalance in these neurotransmitters.

Hypothalamic-Pituitary-Adrenal (HPA) Axis

The intricate mechanism that controls the body's stress response is called the HPA axis. Stress chemicals like cortisol are released when it is engaged. Increased anxiety and panic can be attributed to dysregulation of the HPA axis.

Genetics

There is evidence that suggests panic disorder development is influenced by heredity factors. Although shared

Overcoming Fear and Panic Attacks

environments and social structures also play a role, you may be more susceptible to getting panic disorder if you have a family member who suffers from the condition. According to studies utilising twin and family-based study methods, the hereditability of panic disorder is believed by some to be between 30 and 40 percent. This means that hereditary factors can play a role in some of the risk associated with experiencing panic episodes. Either way, it is more likely that several hereditary variables and not just one gene affect panic episodes. While genetic variations linked to panic disorder are still being identified, it seems that a multitude of genes may be involved in the risk. It is crucial to understand that a person does not automatically get panic disorder or panic attacks just because they have a hereditary susceptibility to these disorders. Life events, environmental variables, and learnt behaviour contribute significantly in triggering panic disorder.

Furthermore, as genetic research in this area is ongoing, more knowledge about the precise genes and pathways behind panic episodes may become available. It is critical to take a comprehensive approach to understanding panic attacks, considering individual variances in coping and resilience in addition to the environmental and hereditary influences. You can seek more precise information and help from a genetic counsellor or healthcare practitioner if you have concerns about panic attacks or a family history of anxiety problems.

Conditioning

Learned associations have the potential to cause certain panic episodes. For instance, if someone comes across, or simply witnesses, someone having a panic attack in a particular setting (like in a lift/elevator or during a flight when escape or the option to move away is not immediately available), they in turn could grow phobic of the setting and get anxious if they are in it again.

Perception and Interpretation of Sensations

Panic might come about subject to how an individual experiences and interprets certain body cues and physical feelings. For example, a panic attack may occur if a primed individual interprets a fast heartbeat as an indication of impending danger without reference to its cause.

External Elements

In individuals who are vulnerable, traumatic experiences, accidents, crime, conflict, long-term stress, and stressful life events can cause panic episodes or contribute to the development of panic disorder.

Brain Circuitry

Studies have demonstrated that a network of brain areas, including the insula, prefrontal cortex, and amygdala, are implicated in the feeling of panic. These brain areas interact and process information about emotional control and threats.

Emotional Aspects

Higher degrees of neuroticism, excessive shyness, pre-existing anxiety, and other specific personality features can all make a person more prone to panic episodes and panic disorder.

Cognitive Elements

Panic symptoms can be made worse by negative thought patterns, such as catastrophic thinking, distrustful outlook, or an increased sense of vulnerability.

Overcoming Fear and Panic Attacks

Developing effective therapies for panic requires a better understanding of the science behind the condition. Ongoing research in this area keeps expanding our knowledge about panic, its origins, and its treatment.

The Role of Neurotransmitters and Neurobiology

Anxiety disorders are multifaceted conditions that are impacted by several neurotransmitters and neurological variables.

An outline of some of the most important elements of the neurobiology and neurotransmitters related to anxiety is provided below:

Neuro-anatomy

The Amygdala.

The processing of emotions, particularly fear and anxiety, is largely dependent on the amygdala. This is a little almond-shaped structure located deep within the brain substance. It can trigger the body's "fight or flight" reaction and is involved in the early identification of possible dangers. It is essential for processing emotions, especially those involving fear, and for controlling the body's stress response. Key functions and characteristics of the amygdala include:

Processing of Emotions

The processing and interpretation of emotions, especially those that are viewed as dangerous or frightening, is greatly facilitated by the amygdala. It enables people to read emotions from the body language and facial expressions of others.

Fear Reaction

The brain's fear circuitry is heavily dependent on the amygdala. The body's "fight or flight" reaction, which causes physiological changes including an elevated heart rate, fast breathing, and the production of stress hormones, can be triggered by the amygdala when a possible threat is perceived.

Memory Consolidation

The processing of emotionally charged memories is aided by the amygdala. It facilitates the storing and retrieval of memories connected to intense emotional events; these may influence actions and reactions in the future.

Emotional Learning

The amygdala contributes to emotional conditioning and learning. It facilitates the brain's ability to link certain inputs or circumstances to feelings, which can have an impact on conduct and judgement.

Social and Interpersonal Functioning

The amygdala plays a role in the processing of social and interpersonal cues in addition to processing fear. It affects social interactions and relationships by assisting in the recognition and response to social cues.

Modulation of Stress Reactions

The amygdala influences the body's stress reactions through interactions with the hypothalamus and prefrontal cortex, besides other brain areas. It assists in controlling the release of stress chemicals like cortisol from the adrenal gland.

Overcoming Fear and Panic Attacks

Threat Identification

The amygdala oversees identifying possible dangers in the surrounding space. It assesses sensory data, such as aural and visual clues, to decide if something is deemed harmful and can do so even at a subconscious level.

Emotion Regulation

The prefrontal cortex, which has connections to the amygdala, has an important function in controlling emotions (even though the amygdala is linked to the production of emotional reactions). Emotional control depends on the amygdala and prefrontal cortex being in balance.

The amygdala is a major participant in many facets of mental health, including anxiety disorders, post-traumatic stress disorder (PTSD), and mood disorders. This is because it is involved in emotional processing and the stress response. The intricacies of the amygdala and its involvement in emotional and psychological processes are still being explored by research. Knowing how the brain regulates emotions and stress reactions requires an insightful understanding of the role of the amygdala.

Prefrontal Cortex

This area of the brain oversees executive processes such as controlling emotions, making decisions, and solving problems. It contributes to anxiety management by regulating the activity of the amygdala. As the most anterior component of the brain's frontal lobes, the prefrontal cortex is essential for a variety of higher-order cognitive processes, emotional control, and sophisticated conduct. It is involved in planning, thinking, personality expression, decision-making, and the regulation of social behaviour.

Here are some of the prefrontal cortex's primary roles and traits:

Executive Function

Because it supervises and regulates a variety of cognitive functions, the prefrontal cortex is frequently referred to as the "executive centre" of the brain. These processes include:

Operational Memory

The capacity to momentarily store and work with information.

Mental Adaptability

The ability to transition between jobs and adjust to changing conditions.

Management of Attention

The capacity to block out distractions and concentrate attention on issues at hand.

The Inhibition of Action

The capacity to restrain or exert control over impulsive actions and reactions.

Making Decisions

The prefrontal cortex is involved in the process of forming decisions. It analyses data from several sources, projects possible outcomes, and helps people make decisions.

Individuality and Social Conduct

The prefrontal cortex has a role in social behaviour regulation and personality formation. It supports moral judgement, empathy, emotional control, and the capacity to consider the thoughts and feelings of others.

Decide and Establish Goals

This area of the brain aids with action planning and organisation for long-term objectives. It also helps to divide difficult jobs into smaller, more manageable segments.

Control of Emotions

The amygdala and other brain areas interact with the prefrontal cortex to control emotional reactions. It can help people adjust to emotionally charged circumstances by regulating the strength and duration of emotional reactions.

Activating Memory

To execute cognitive activities, working memory requires storing and modifying information momentarily. The functioning of working memory processes depends on the prefrontal cortex.

Language Interpreting

Higher-order language processes, such as semantic processing and language creation, are facilitated by the prefrontal cortex, especially the left prefrontal cortex, as in most people language processing mostly takes place in the left hemisphere of the brain.

Solution-Selection

The prefrontal cortex helps with complicated problem solving by assessing possible solutions, balancing benefits, and drawbacks, and deciding on the best course of action.

Self-knowledge

It contributes to self-awareness by enabling people to consider their feelings, ideas, and actions. Personal development and self-regulation depend on having this self-awareness.

Personality Disorders

A few psychiatric conditions, such as mood disorders, attention-deficit and hyperactivity disorder (ADHD), schizophrenia, and other personality disorders, have all been linked to dysfunction in the prefrontal cortex.

Development and Maturation

During adolescence and the early years of adulthood, the prefrontal cortex keeps growing and changing. Improvements in impulse control, cognitive control, and decision-making at this time have all been connected to this process.

Executive function, emotional regulation, and social behaviour deficiencies can result from injury or dysfunction to the prefrontal cortex. In neuroscience, psychology, and psychiatry, comprehending the function of the prefrontal cortex is essential because it offers insights into a range of cognitive and behavioural problems. This aids in the creation of treatment strategies.

Chemical Messengers

Gamma-Aminobutyric Acid (GABA) is a neurotransmitter that acts as an inhibitor and lowers the excitability of individual brain cells or neurons. It helps to regulate anxiety by having a relaxing impact on the brain. Elevated anxiety is correlated with reduced GABA levels.

Overcoming Fear and Panic Attacks

One other neurotransmitter that affects mood, emotion, and conduct is serotonin. Anxiety disorders and low serotonin levels have been related. By boosting serotonin availability in the brain, selective serotonin reuptake inhibitors (SSRIs), a family of drugs often prescribed as antidepressants, can also be used to alleviate anxiety.

The neurotransmitter noradrenaline is a component of the body's stress response. Anxiety and elevated arousal are linked to increased noradrenaline activity. Noradrenaline receptor blockers have the potential to lessen anxiety symptoms.

Dopamine is involved in the brain's reward and pleasure circuits. According to some studies, certain anxiety disorders may be associated with changes in dopamine function.

The excitatory neurotransmitter glutamate is involved in the brain's signal transmission process. Disorders related to anxiety have been linked to dysregulation of glutamate signalling.

Hypothalamic-Pituitary-Adrenal (HPA) Axis

The neuroendocrine system known as the HPA axis controls how the body reacts to stress. The HPA axis releases the stress hormone cortisol under stressful situations. Anxiety disorders can be exacerbated by dysregulation of the HPA axis. This can be seen in cases of tumours such as pheochromocytomas, and/or chronic cortisol exposure.

Brain Circuitry

The insula, anterior cingulate cortex, prefrontal cortex, and amygdala are among the brain circuits linked to anxiety.

These brain areas interact and process information about identifying threats and controlling emotions. Neuroplasticity, or alterations in the structure and function of the brain, is involved in the emergence and maintenance of anxiety disorders. Anxiety and stress can gradually change the way the brain functions.

It is essential to grasp the neurobiology and neurotransmitters associated with anxiety to create successful treatment plans. To reduce anxiety feelings, medications like beta-blockers, benzodiazepines, and SSRIs as well as psychotherapy techniques like CBT are today used to address these neurobiological variables. This area of study is constantly expanding our knowledge of anxiety and how to cure it.

A person's physical attributes, habits, and susceptibility to certain conditions, such as mental health problems like anxiety, depression, and schizophrenia, are all influenced by both hereditary genetic and environmental variables.

An outline of the ways in which these two influence various elements is provided below:

Genetic Elements

Inherited qualities. An individual's genetic composition determines several qualities, including height, hair texture, and eye colour. Usually, genetic inheritance passes these features down from one's biological parents.

Hereditary Predisposition

There is a hereditary component to some ailments, such as mental health problems like depression and anxiety. Due to shared genetic characteristics, those who have a family history of certain conditions may be more susceptible to acquiring them.

Overcoming Fear and Panic Attacks

Gene Variants

Certain gene variants, or alleles, might make a person more susceptible to certain conditions. For instance, schizophrenia, bipolar illness, and autism spectrum disorders are linked to hereditary risk factors. Although they can make a person more vulnerable, these gene variations do not necessarily lead to such conditions.

Gene-Environment Interactions

Genetic or environmental variables can interact to affect behaviour and health. For example, an excessively calorific diet and sedentary lifestyle may exacerbate a hereditary susceptibility to fat. On the other hand, when a child observes an adult family member expressing a certain phobia, this may pass on that phobia to that child.

External Elements

Early Life Distress

A person's growth and mental health can be significantly impacted by their upbringing and experiences throughout their formative years. Adverse childhood experiences (ACEs), such as abuse, neglect, or other traumatic events might raise an individual's lifetime risk of developing mental health issues.

Stress

Long-term stressors, such as tension from the workplace, money problems, or interpersonal problems, can cause or exacerbate mental health disorders including depression and anxiety.

Physical Environment

A person's physical and mental health can be impacted by environmental variables such as pollution, too little sunlight, excessive heat or cold, and access to natural open non-urbanised green areas like parks and woodlands.

Social Environment

Social elements are vital to mental health and wellbeing. These elements include family connections, social support, and community. Good social relationships can serve as barriers against mental health issues.

Social and Cultural Influences

Stigma, discrimination, harsh cultural norms, and high social expectations may all influence one's mental health. People who experience prejudice, for instance, may be more vulnerable to mental health issues.

Lifestyle Decisions

Individual habits including eating habits, exercise routines, drug usage, and sleep habits can have a big influence on one's physical and emotional well-being.

Trauma

Post-traumatic stress disorder (PTSD) and other mental health conditions can result from exposure to traumatic events, such as violent crimes, accidents, war, or natural disasters.

It is crucial to remember that there are many factors interacting between hereditary and environmental influences. Not everyone exposed to environmental risk factors will

Overcoming Fear and Panic Attacks

suffer unfavourable effects, and not everyone with a genetic tendency will acquire a particular ailment. The effects of both genetic and environmental variables on health and well-being can be lessened by resilience, protective factors, and access to the right treatments and support.

By using knowledge from disciplines including genetics, psychology, and public health, an understanding of the interaction between hereditary and environmental variables can be derived. This in turn can be used for the development of methods for illness prevention and treatment as well as the promotion of general health and wellbeing.

As stated earlier, panic attacks with abrupt and severe episodes of great dread or anxiety, accompanied by physical symptoms, are the hallmarks of panic attacks. Although panic attacks have many characteristics in common, their causes and particular symptoms may vary.

Accordingly, there are several categories of panic attacks.

Expected (Cued) Panic Attacks

These attacks take place in reaction to a predetermined trigger(s). The attack is anticipated as it is associated with a particular phobia or dread. Specific phobias such as a fear of flying or a dread of public speaking. In addition, the cue maybe trauma-related signals (such as recollections of a traumatic incident). The causes of cued panic attacks might be easier to identify than those of unexpected ones.

Unexpected (Un-cued) Panic Attacks

These episodes of terror strike without warning and without a clear external cause. They can occur at any time, even when you're sleeping or unwinding. People who have un-cued panic episodes frequently worry that they will occur at any time, which can lead to the development of panic disorder.

Panic Attacks Bound by Situations

These panic episodes are strongly associated with a particular scenario of events. They always happen when someone is in or expects to be in a specific setting or situation. For instance, a person may often get panic attacks when using lifts or giving a speech in front of a particular group or audience.

Panic Attacks that are Situationally Inclined

Although these attacks are more prone to happen in particular circumstances, they do not always occur consistently when a person is in those circumstances. For example, a person may not always have panic episodes when flying. Panic may happen only occasionally.

Panic Attacks that Happen at Night

People who have nocturnal panic attacks typically wake up from their sleep in a condition of extreme fear and dread. It is possible that nocturnal panic attack sufferers will not always recall the precise details of nightmares or dreams that can set them off.

Limited-Symptom Panic Attacks

Compared to a full-blown panic attack, a panic attack may occasionally exhibit less or other symptoms. Angina, vertigo, and dyspnoea (breathlessness) are a few examples of the panic symptoms that might be present during these limited-symptom episodes. Even panic attacks with few symptoms can be upsetting and unpleasant, particularly if they happen frequently.

It is noteworthy that the differentiation between these

Overcoming Fear and Panic Attacks

categories of panic episodes is not invariably strict, and certain individuals may encounter a blend of them. Quality of life can be greatly impacted by panic episodes, which can be an indication of panic disorder or other anxiety disorders. Effective treatment can help people manage and lessen the frequency and severity of panic attacks. This may involve counselling and, in certain circumstances, medication.

Role of the Amygdala in the Fight-or-Flight Response

The processing of emotions, especially those associated with fear and the initiation of the fight-or-flight response, is mostly controlled by the amygdala. A perceived threat or danger triggers the body's fight-or-flight response, a physiological and psychological reaction that primes the body to either confront the threat (fight) or escape it (flight). The fight-or-flight reflex and the amygdala are linked in the following ways:

Identifying Threats

The brain's deep-seated amygdala, situated in the temporal lobes, oversees identifying possible threats or dangers in the surrounding environment. It accomplishes this by processing signals from inside the body that are connected to emotional states as well as sensory data from the outside environment, such as visual and auditory stimuli.

Emotional Processing

The amygdala analyses information and determines the emotional importance of any possible danger. It can quickly determine whether a stimulus is possibly harmful and set off an appropriate emotional reaction.

Activation of the Sympathetic Nervous System

The sympathetic nervous system of the body is triggered by signals sent by the amygdala, which evaluates a danger as serious. Numerous physiological alterations result from this, including:

- Elevated blood pressure and heart rate (palpitations).
- Breathing quickly to improve oxygen intake.
- Dilated pupils to enhance visual clarity.
- Blood flow redirected to the muscles, readying them for action.
- Elevated sensory sensitivity and heightened attentiveness, to allow for an early response.

Release of Stress Hormones

The hypothalamus, which receives communication from the amygdala, via the hypothalamus and pituitary gland instructs the adrenal glands to release stress hormones, mainly noradrenaline and adrenaline. These hormones boost energy and attention, further priming the body for action.

Emotional Reaction

The amygdala causes emotional reactions like dread, anxiety, or rage in tandem with the physiological changes. These feelings may inspire someone to face the danger head-on or look for other ways to escape or avoid it.

Making Decisions

In reaction to a perceived threat, decisions are influenced by the amygdala's function in assessing threats and emotional processing. Without much conscious thought, it might trigger quick, automatic reactions like fighting or running.

Overcoming Fear and Panic Attacks

The fight-or-flight response is an evolutionary response developed to help humans and other animals respond rapidly to potentially fatal situations. Although this reaction is important in emergency situations, it may also be overstretched to include perceived dangers or improperly provoked stimulations, which can result in persistent stress, anxiety disorders, and post-traumatic stress disorder (PTSD).

Appreciating how the brain and body react to stress and perceived threat requires an understanding of the role played by the amygdala in the fight-or-flight response. The therapeutic management and mindset change approach recommend in this book can be employed to reduce the negative effects of excessive or improper activation of this response on mental and physical wellbeing.

CHAPTER 2

IDENTIFYING AND CATEGORISING PANIC ATTACKS

DIAGNOSIS AND ASSESSMENT

Further observations on the Fight-or-Flight Reaction

As stated earlier, the reaction is a crucial physiological response often referred to as the stress response, and it has been essential for the survival and evolution of our species. When danger approaches, this natural reaction gets triggered, readying the body to either confront or avoid that danger. Due to the many challenges and situations faced by our ancestors over time, the fight-or-flight response has undergone significant evolutionary modifications over the millennia.

The Origins of the Fight or Flight Reaction

The reaction was first recognised in the earliest vertebrates, who acquired basic stress reflexes to ward off predators or snare prey. As vertebrate species multiplied and experienced evolutionary change, these basic stress responses evolved into more complex forms. As reptiles had better developed brains and hormonal defences against threats, their emergence marked a turning point in the evolution of this system. This reptilian evolution is represented in our own central nervous system's limbic system. The limbic system is involved in all behaviours needed for survival, such as feeding, reproduction, caring for our young and of course our fight or flight response. There are some who use the phrase "lizard brain" to depict a severe response to fear, highlighting a similarity to the animal, and in particular it freezing up in response to fear since it is about all a lizard has in brain function.

The Origin of the Sympathetic Nervous System and Evolution of Mammals

Mammalian evolution further refined the fight-or-flight response. One of the most significant developments was the creation of the sympathetic nervous system (SNS), which oversees mobilising the body's resources under stressful conditions. The SNS and other stress hormones produce adrenaline, which raises heart rate, increases brain activity, and directs blood flow to muscles and other organs.

Mammals, for example, have highly developed brains and utilise limbic systems to process emotions. The fight-or-flight response incorporated fear and anxiety into these systems, allowing for a more distinctive and rapid response to threats. Additionally, mammals developed the ability to adapt to changing circumstances and learn from past mistakes and interactions, which improved their odds of surviving.

Primates Effect on Social Complexity and Cognitive Adaptations

As primates evolved, the fight-or-flight response adapted to the demands of more complex social environments. Primate connections with other members of their species are very important since they are in general gregarious animals. Members of different species often cooperate, compete, and have complex hierarchies. Social complexity influenced the development of more sophisticated cognitive abilities, which in turn influenced the stress response.

Human Evolution and Contemporary Stress Reaction

The evolutionary process that resulted in Homo sapiens further refining the fight-or-flight response, came about when we evolved the ability for higher order reasoning and decision-making in the prefrontal brain. This allowed us to consider choices other than fighting or escaping, and to assess threats with greater objectivity.

In humans, the fight-or-flight reaction became entwined with social dynamics. People found that the stress reaction helped them cope not just with physical threats but also with challenging social situations. The ability to detect and react appropriately to social cues became critical to survival, since conflicts and alliances within a group may have a significant impact on an individual's chances of surviving. For example, imagine the risk of working in the court of the Roman Emperor Tiberius or Caligula, if the reputation of their vicious nature is justified. One situational misstep and your survival could be suddenly and violently terminated.

Although the fight-or-flight response is still necessary for human existence in the modern world. Today it is often triggered by less life-threatening stressors such as work deadlines, traffic congestion, accidents, or social conflict. Though these situations elicit the same physiological responses as real threats, our ability to think and adapt gives us more control over how we respond.

The fight-or-flight reaction was shaped by the struggles our ancestors faced through millions of years of evolution. Even

Overcoming Fear and Panic Attacks

if the contemporary world brings with it new stressors, we have learned to utilise reason to control and adapt this response to a range of situations. Comprehending the evolution of the fight-or-flight response offers us a window into the life of our ancestors and helps us overcome challenges that lie ahead. It is for this very reason that the inappropriate firing of the fight-or-flight response, with no obvious tangible danger in the vicinity, causes such dread and mental confusion.

Appreciating that the "fight-or-flight" response can be both a trigger of attacks of panic and can also be triggered by them, while at the same time grasping the complexities of the reaction itself, can be extremely challenging.
Much of the treatment for panic disorder and anxiety in general is somewhat focused of controlling and managing this overwhelming reaction when it occurs inappropriately.

Methods for Identifying and Assessing Panic

When diagnosing panic disorder, mental health providers do a thorough examination that includes a detailed analysis of the patient's symptoms, medical background, and psychological history. The Diagnostic and Statistical handbook of Mental problems (DSM-5), a widely used diagnostic handbook for mental health problems, contains criteria that are frequently followed during the diagnosis process.

When diagnosing panic disorder, mental health practitioners take the following steps:

The Clinical Interview

A clinical interview is frequently the first step in the

diagnostic procedure. The person seeking help and treatment will be questioned about the kind, length, and frequency of panic attacks, among other symptoms. They can ask about any circumstances or triggers that cause panic attacks, as well as any accompanying mental or physical symptoms.

Medical and Psychological History

The mental health practitioner will inquire about the patient's medical background, including any pertinent drug and alcohol usage, physical health issues, and medical disorders. A psychiatric history is evaluated as well, encompassing any previous or ongoing diagnoses, family history and treatments related to mental health.

Differential Diagnosis

The doctor will look for other illnesses that can cause similar symptoms, such as substance-induced anxiety, physical abnormalities (such as heart, adrenal or thyroid issues), or other anxiety inducing physical disorders.

Diagnostic Guidelines

The doctor will determine if the patient satisfies the DSM-5 criteria to diagnose panic disorder. This comprises the following:

- Recurrent unexpected panic attacks
  Constant fear or concern about potential future attacks or marked behavioural changes after at least two unexpected panic episodes.

- Lack of a particular trigger or circumstance
  That is to say, there is no reliable correlation between panic attacks and a particular phobia or circumstance.

Overcoming Fear and Panic Attacks

- Significant distress or impairment
  Significant distress or impairment in day-to-day living is brought on by panic episodes, associated fears, and avoidance behaviours.

Assessment Instruments

To obtain more data on the intensity and significance of panic disorder symptoms, mental health practitioners may employ standardised assessment instruments and questionnaires. These instruments support the tracking of treatment efficacy.

Rule Out other Conditions

To treat panic disorder, the doctor will rule out any other psychological or physical illnesses that can exacerbate it or resemble it. This might entail medical testing or physical examinations.

Duration and Course

The persistence of panic episodes and associated symptoms for a minimum of one month is a crucial need for the diagnosis of panic disorder. To ascertain if the disorder satisfies this requirement, the doctor will evaluate the length and trajectory of the disorder.

Functional Impairment

The therapist will evaluate how the patient's panic disorder impacts their day-to-day activities, such as their job, interpersonal interactions, and general quality of life.

Treatment Planning

Following a diagnosis, the mental health specialist will work together with the patient to create an individualised treatment plan. Psychotherapy, such as cognitive behavioural counselling, and medication may be part of this plan.

If you think you may have panic disorder or any other mental health condition, it is critical to have a comprehensive assessment and diagnosis from a licenced psychiatric health professional. Panic disorder may be substantially better managed, and patients can reclaim control of their life with a prompt diagnosis and appropriate therapy.

Tools for Self-Evaluation

Self-assessment tools are forms of questionnaires, checklists, or other instruments that people may use to measure and consider different facets of their mental health, personality, well-being, or problems. These resources might be helpful for understanding one's own ideas, emotions, actions, and general way of being. But to be clear, they should, however, be used in addition to professional examination and diagnosis, and are not substitutes of them.

Here are a few self-assessment resources for a range of uses:

▪ Generalised Anxiety Disorder 7

Generalised Anxiety Disorder 7 (GAD-7) is an extensively used self-assessment instrument to gauge the intensity of anxiety symptoms.

▪ Patient Health Questionnaire 9

The Patient Health Questionnaire 9 (PHQ-9) evaluates the degree and occurrence of depression symptoms and feelings.

▪ Perceived Stress Scale

The Perceived Stress Scale (PSS) gauges how much stress

Overcoming Fear and Panic Attacks

people feel in their day-to-day lives.

▪ Wellness Wheel

Assists people in evaluating their physical, emotional, social, and environmental well-being, among other aspects of their overall health.

▪ Psychology and Personality

Openness, conscientiousness, extraversion, agreeableness, and neuroticism are among the Big Five Personality Traits, which may be assessed by self-evaluation.

▪ Myers-Briggs Type Indicator

The well-known Myers-Briggs Type Indicator (MBTI) divides personality types into groups according to preferences for things like extraversion vs introversion and thinking versus emotion.

▪ The Enneagram Test

This test uses nine interrelated personality types to assess personality traits.

▪ Attachment Style Questionnaires

These evaluate several kinds of connections in relationships, including avoidant, anxious, and secure. People may learn more about their major intimacy languages and how to express closeness in relationships using this questionnaire.

▪ Substances Abuse and Addiction

- o The Alcohol Use Disorders Identification Test (AUDIT). Evaluates the hazards associated with alcohol usage.

- o Drug Abuse Screening Test (DAST). Assesses drug usage and its effects on health and wellbeing.

- **Food Abuse Disorders**

Eating Attitudes Test (EAT-26)
Examines potential eating problem signs and symptoms.

- **body shape Image Questionnaires**

There are several instruments available to evaluate how well one feels regarding their physical appearance.

- **Child Rearing**

- o Parenting Stress Index (PSI) Evaluates parental-related stressors and stress levels.

- o The Parent-Child Interaction Questionnaire (PCIT-Q) assesses the quality of relationships and parent-child interactions.

- **Job and Profession**

Tools for Career Assessment
A variety of tests, like the Holland Codes and the Strong Interest Inventory, assist people in determining their preferences and areas of interest in the workplace.

- **Tools for Assessing Burnout**

The Maslach Burnout Inventory is one tool that may be used to measure the amount of burnout in the workplace.

- **Overall, Health and Life Contentment**

Overcoming Fear and Panic Attacks

Overall life satisfaction is measured using the Satisfaction with Life Scale (SWLS).

- **Resilience Questionnaires**

Evaluate a person's capacity to handle pressure and hardship. Appreciate that although self-assessment instruments might offer significant perspectives, they cannot replace expert assessment and diagnosis. Consult a licenced mental health professional for advice and direction if you are worried about your psychological state or well-being. They provide individualised assessment and support. Self-assessment instruments should only be used in combination with expert advice, but they may be a useful place to start when it comes to self-awareness and personal growth.

The Significance of Obtaining Expert Assistance

To avoid any doubt, this book stipulates that it is crucial to seek assistance from professionals when dealing with psychological disorders, and this is for the following reasons:

❖ Precise Diagnosis

Early accurate diagnosis for any illness is a must in order to expedite treatment. Mental health practitioners, such as psychologists, psychiatrists, therapists, and counsellors, have been trained to carry out thorough evaluations and offer precise diagnoses. They can ascertain the existence, nature, and severity of a mental health issue in each case and give correct guidance moving forward.

❖ Tailored Care

Mental health professionals create individualised treatment regimens once a diagnosis has been made. Evidence-based treatments and, where necessary, pharmaceutical management are frequently included in these plans. Customised therapies are more successful in meeting the specific needs of each patient, thus minimising patient suffering.

❖ Symptom Management

Mental health specialists can assist people in controlling and reducing uncomfortable symptoms. This might involve lowering anxiety levels, controlling depressive symptoms, dealing with mood fluctuations, developing coping mechanisms, and boosting general wellbeing.

❖ Early Intervention and Control

By obtaining professional assistance as soon as possible, mental health issues can be kept from getting worse. A decreased likelihood of complications and better therapeutic results with less side effects are frequently linked to early intervention.

❖ Acquiring Coping Skills

Mental health professionals impart useful information and instruction regarding coping mechanisms and approaches to better handle stress, anxiety, and other difficulties. These can play a key role in enhancing one's capacity to manage many challenging circumstances and thoughts.

❖ Support and Validation

When people share their ideas and emotions with professionals they do so in a safe, non-judgemental, and understanding and accepting space. In many cases it is easier

Overcoming Fear and Panic Attacks

to confide in professionals rather than close friends and family. The sense of empowerment that comes from such validation can reduce their sense of loneliness and isolation that many patients endure.

❖ Medication Management

Psychiatrists can prescribe and oversee the use of medications, ensuring their safe and effective usage, when they are a component of the treatment plan. They will help avoid any harmful post treatment complications or dangerous drug interactions associated with such medications.

❖ Therapeutic Relationships

Building a therapeutic relationship with a trusted healthcare professional in the field of mental health can offer a secure conduit for self-examination and recovery. Confidentiality, empathy, and trust are the cornerstones of such a partnership.

❖ Safety Planning

Behavioural health experts can quickly create safety plans and securely link people who are at risk of suicide or self-harm with the proper crisis response services.

❖ Removing Stigma

People who actively seek assistance and share their experiences help lessen the stigma associated with mental health. Breaking down barriers and motivating other people to get treatment are achieved by openly discussing and addressing mental health issues.

❖ Long-Term Well-Being

Promoting long-term well-being is an important aspect of mental health therapy, in addition to symptom relief. It can support people in developing resilience, self-worth, and an optimistic attitude on life.

❖ Family and Social Support

Receiving professional assistance will be advantageous for the individual as well as their close relatives. A more supportive and communicative atmosphere may be created via family counselling and education, which will facilitate rapid rehabilitation.

In conclusion, obtaining expert assistance for mental health issues is an assertive and enabling measure towards overall wellness. It is a marker of fortitude, self-knowledge, and self-care. An individual's life can be significantly improved by receiving professional care, whether they are coping with a specific mental health issue or are confronting other obstacles.

Differentiating Between Panic Attacks and Other Conditions

Since certain symptoms of panic attacks may coincide with those of other health concerns, it can be difficult to distinguish panic attacks from other disorders or medical issues. But here is a recap of a few crucial elements that might help distinguish panic attacks disorder from other illnesses:

Unexpected Onset

Most panic episodes start off unexpectedly and climax a few minutes later. They can be distinguished from many other

Overcoming Fear and Panic Attacks

medical or psychiatric problems by their abrupt and acute onset.

Severe Fear or Discomfort

Severe fear, dread, or discomfort are hallmarks of panic episodes. The worry is disproportionate to the circumstances and is usually coupled with a sense of approaching danger.

Duration

Panic episodes usually last no more than ten to twenty minutes. Extended duration of symptoms may be observed in other medical diseases or concerns.

Stress or Worry

Stress, worry, or certain circumstances that are perceived as threatening or frightening can all set off a panic attack. Separating panic attacks from other disorders can be made easier by being aware of the triggers involved.

Recurrent Episodes

When a person has frequent panic attacks and is consumed by the worry of experiencing further episodes, it is determined that they have panic disorder. Having frequent, unplanned panic attacks is a crucial requirement.

Elimination of Medical Causes

It is critical to rule out any underlying illnesses that can be mistaken for panic attack symptoms. Panic attacks can be an indication of conditions including drug withdrawal, respiratory illnesses, cardiac difficulties, and thyroid or adrenal problems. A comprehensive medical assessment can assist in ruling out such causes.

Reaction to Medication or Relaxation

Medication or relaxation techniques intended to lessen anxiety and panic are frequently effective in preventing panic attacks. If using relaxation or focussed anti-anxiety medicine considerably reduces symptoms, it may indicate that the episodes are panic attacks.

Overall Clinical Picture

To arrive at an appropriate diagnosis, mental health experts consider the patient's full history, symptoms, and the environment in which those symptoms manifest. It is crucial to remember that people who have symptoms akin to panic attacks ought to get a full assessment from a medical expert or mental health specialist to ascertain the underlying reason(s). For any medical or psychological condition to be properly treated, a proper medically supervised diagnosis is essential to creating an effective treatment strategy.

CHAPTER 3

MANAGING AND TREATING PANIC ATTACKS

Developing the ability to regulate and handle what is happening to you during a panic attack is the first step towards managing these episodes in the future. As mentioned earlier, the attacks can happen in a range of different circumstances resulting in marked distress as well as an avoidance behaviour wrongly intended to prevent such attacks in the future.

Most people who suffer a panic attack for the first time are under the age of twenty-five. Leading up to the event they would have been under stress for some time, but many still identify a particular difficult event or challenge that, they believe, acted as the proverbial "straw" that broke the camel's back and set-off the panic attack(s).

It is critical to understand and appreciate the fact that panic attacks are not correlated with insanity or a threat to life. Knowing this early will greatly reduce the initial and incessant fear and dread. I would even go further and contend that those who suffer from panic attacks are not even candidates to go insane, and yet insanity is very regularly the main fear for most panic attack sufferers.

It is important to recognise that individuals who have experienced panic attacks possess a heightened and often distressing awareness of the many life stressors and pressures that encompass their existence. The observation that they have such a heightened sense of concern about these matters only serves to emphasise its veracity.

One will very quickly conclude, when meeting a truly insane patient, that self-awareness and dealing with daily stresses and reality in general, is not an issue for those who go insane. Those who are unfortunate enough to suffer from the reality-detached state that is insanity, are usually oblivious to what surrounds them. They are mostly living in their own world, and the burden of suffering that accompanies this illness is mainly shouldered by the patient's family rather than the patient himself.

When evaluating challenging life situations, keep in mind that when it comes to psychologically stressful life events, their impact can be quite subjective. The effect of a situation can vary widely from person to person, i.e. it is possible that something that would cause me to feel substantial psychological stress may be quite straightforward for you, and vice versa.

When trying to identify candidates that may develop panic attacks, I am of the firm belief that, given the right set of circumstances, panic attacks could affect any one of us.
If you were to visualise your frame of mind or psyche as a solid brick wall or fortification. That brick wall will invariably contain some fragile bricks hidden within the wall's fabric.
Each person may have a different number of fragile bricks in their psyche, but even in the most resilient amongst us, there will invariably be a few such bricks embedded in their mental fortification. Should stressful circumstances assemble in such a way that they would so much as just gently tap one such fragile brick, then the whole psychological wall may wane, and panic could ensue.

Overcoming Fear and Panic Attacks

What Does an Individual Undergo when Suffering a Panic Attack

When a panic attack happens for the first time it may cause you to experience all the unpleasant symptoms mentioned in earlier chapters. Your body is behaving as if it is reacting to a dangerous animal in the room, or some other life-threatening situation. This will cause an instant conflict between what the mind can reason and substantiate and how the body is reacting or sensing.

Commonly, initial thoughts are, "What's going on with me?", "Can I die, or will I lose my mind and go insane?".
You feel like you are rapidly losing control of yourself, and you try desperately to get that control back, but you cannot seem to make that happen. Even when the fear eventually starts to subside, it is clear that it does so independent of your control efforts. At this stage, more recurrences are probable; and if the panic attack is not treated quickly, panic disorder may arise.

After the event, many patients find the panic attack to be quite humiliating and start to feel guilty for acting so timidly in the face of the terror they felt. Those feeling shame frequently decide not to tell friends and family about the occurrence, with the rare exception of confiding in parents or elder siblings, whom they believe will be more sympathetic than judgmental.

The body reacts to the panic situation by releasing the "fight-or-flight" compounds, adrenaline, noradrenaline, and cortisol. The more times this happens, the body is said to become sensitised to these substances. Thereinafter, whenever a trigger releases even a tiny quantity of these hormones into the bloodstream, it results in further panic attacks. The sufferer quickly realises that there are many triggers that can cause such hormone release to occur, and that they have no influence over the moment and/or place of that release.

To further add to the burden, the dismay one feels from the prospect that people may actually sense or see the manifestations of the panic attacks in a social setting or gatherings, making them appear foolish in front of onlookers, makes the whole issue so much harder. This forces one into a situation where one begins to "fear the fear itself."

Up until now, you have been somewhat powerless to combat your terror. You feel you have little or no control over it; and it comes and goes as it pleases.

This is now going to DRASTICALLY change.

Mindset and Concept Lock-In Needed to Manage Panic

We know that people with a wide range of personality traits can be affected by anxiety and panic disorder. Panic is not usually specific to any one personality type. Panic may be influenced by a large a variety of elements such as, genetic inheritance, upbringing, and difficult life experiences. These can all influence an individual's susceptibility to the development of panic.

However, there may be an increased association between certain personality characteristics and attributes and individuals who suffer from anxiety and panic disorders.
Anxiety and panic disorder sufferers frequently exhibit perfectionist tendencies and a strong drive not to fail. They may be micro-managers to prevent making mistakes and

Overcoming Fear and Panic Attacks

avoiding any form of humiliation and they are quite hard and unforgiving of themselves. Recurring concerns and ruminating thoughts are characteristic of anxiety disorder sufferers. Individuals can often find themselves thinking in terms of difficult and complex speculative circumstances and worst-case scenarios. These traits will need to be addressed in the longer term to keep one panic free.

The essential concept lock-in and mindset to control panic is specific and quite straightforward. In the immediate term, you must change your approach for how you try to handle your panic episodes.

As you will remember, I said that as soon as you experience the first panic attack, you intuitively attempt to take back control of your emotional state and fight to regain your thought equilibrium. What you must now learn, is to take the complete opposite approach to that intuitive response, since it is there that your long-term solution is to be found.

Instead of trying to fight what panic is doing to you, you must deliberately give in to it. You must get yourself into the mindset that chooses not to fight anymore.

To help you do this, you must develop an inner dialogue where you speak directly to your panic with resolve and look it straight in the eye so to speak. You must assuredly accept anything that comes your way from this act of mental acquiescence. You will tell your panic, "You won't drive me insane, or harm me in any way, and in any case if you could, I wouldn't want to live with such a weak mind or body". You must communicate to yourself the understanding that panic is not all powerful, as you once thought, and then knowingly and purposefully decide not to fight or resist it.

This must be your inner monologue throughout the panic

attack. Once you succeed in mentally stepping away from the fight your mind will relax. Your body's fight-or-flight hormones will cease to be produced, breaking the vicious cycle that has been causing your emotional upheaval and the panic will begin to fade away.

You may be surprised to know that later, as your confidence grows, you will even begin to bait the panic and tell it to "bring it on" but still you will disregard and not resist it. In essence, you will continue to firmly stand up to this mental bully by simply refusing to fight or battle it.

The first time you try this, you will not succeed completely, but you will feel, even if just for a moment, a small withdrawal or retreat of the panic attack. With that brief retreat, you will realise that for the first time that you can indeed influence and get the better of this condition and that you are no longer defenceless and without a weapon.

Note that implementing this advice will require some fortitude, practice, and discipline. You will need to practice some of the exercises and techniques described in this book to help calm your mind and better prepare you to take on panic in this way. Rest assured that the principle is sound and the method extremely effective.

By applying this methodology one can gradually and successfully regained control, and I have no doubt that you too will accomplish this goal.

Remember that it is your dedication and practise that will dictate how quickly you reach your purpose. The reader will need to supplement the effort with exercises that better calm the mind before confronting panic in the manner described.

I will now go through some supplementary methods and

Overcoming Fear and Panic Attacks

strategies that will help and support in the mind-set alteration effort.

Supplementary Methods and Exercises

A variety of techniques can be used to help manage panic attacks, with the unified goal being to lessen the severity and frequency of panic episodes as well as improve one's ability to handle the symptoms when they arise.

Here are some practical methods to help focus one's thoughts and calm the mind:

Deep Breathing

A straightforward yet powerful method for controlling and lowering anxiety. It is a technique for relaxation that involves breathing deeply and slowly to reduce tension and encourage tranquilly and calm.

It helps in several ways:

Nervous System Soothing

The parasympathetic nerve system, also known as the "rest and digest" system, can be triggered by deep breathing. In doing so, the sympathetic nervous system's "fight-or-flight" reaction causing tension and anxiety is better dissipated.

Easing of Tense Muscles

Physical discomfort from tense muscles is a common symptom of anxiety. The physical signs of worry are lessened by deep breathing and focus, which also helps to relax stiff muscles. Mental and physical tension feed off each other.

Decreasing Heart Rate

One typical sign of anxiety and panic is a sudden pounding and accelerated heart rate, which may be slowed with deep, steady breathing.

Upregulating Intake of Oxygen

Ingesting more oxygen through deep breathing can enhance cognitive performance and lessen anxiety perception.

Practice Deep Breathing

Locate an Appropriate Place

To engage in deep breathing exercises, locate a peaceful, comfortable area free from distractions.

Find a Comfortable Position

You can either lie down or sit upright. Just make sure you assume a comfortable posture. It might be more beneficial to practise after taking a warm bath or shower. Your body's residual surface moisture will help increase awareness of your physical senses.

Have Your Eyes Closed (optional)

You may decrease distractions and concentrate more on your breathing by closing your eyes. Note that this may not suit everyone, so do what gives you most comfort.

Slowly Breath in and Hold your Breath

Inhale deeply and slowly through your nose. Clear your mind of any thoughts and simply concentrate on counting each breath and the action of fully filling your lungs while you

Overcoming Fear and Panic Attacks

breathe. As you inhale, you should feel your abdomen rise. Try imagining the air filling your lungs, passing via your nose, throat, trachea, to enter your lungs. Next, exhale slowly and again imagine and follow the air out of your lungs and body in reverse order.

Hold your breath at the peak of your inspiration without straining. Breathe out gently releasing all your stress as the air leaves through your mouth or nose. You may try the 4-7-8 technique. Inhale for a count of 4, hold your breath for 7, and exhale for a count of 8.

Repeat this for several breathing cycles.

Practice this daily, always focussing on counting your breaths as well. Seek a duration of ten to thirty minutes, according to your comfort level and available time.
To fully benefit from deep breathing, regular practise is essential. It should become a part of your regular daily regimen and can be used as required when you're stressed or anxious.

Keep in mind that there are several relaxation methods for handling anxiety, deep breathing being only one of them. It can be utilised alone or in combination with other methods of relaxation including progressive muscle relaxation, guided imagery, or mindfulness meditation. Try out a variety of methods to see which ones help you reduce anxiety most and cultivate a sense of peace and wellbeing.

Progressive Muscle Relaxation

One very useful method for lowering tension and anxiety is progressive muscle relaxation, or PMR. It entails focussing and methodically mentally relaxing various bodily muscle groups, which promotes both mental and physical relaxation.

The foundation of PMR is the idea that physical relaxation can aid in bringing about a sense of mental calm and lessen the bodily manifestations of worry.

PMR reduces anxiety by:

Easing Tense Muscles

Physical discomfort from tense muscles is a common symptom of anxiety. By assisting people in noticing and letting go of this tension, PMR encourages relaxation. The mind-body link is improved through PMR. People can become more connected to their bodies and experience a grounding and soothing effect by concentrating on the bodily feelings of tension and relaxation.

Activating the Parasympathetic Nervous System

PMR activates the body's parasympathetic nervous system, counteracts the "fight-or-flight" stress response and induces a state of relaxation.

Practicing Progressive Muscle Relaxation

Locate a Peaceful Area

Select a tranquil, comfortable area free from interruptions.

Take a Comfortable Position

PMR can be performed in a variety of positions, including sitting, lying down on a bed or yoga mat, or even standing.

Have Your Eyes Closed (optional)

You can lessen distractions and concentrate more on the

Overcoming Fear and Panic Attacks

bodily experiences by closing your eyes if that suits you.

Methodically Power Down and Relax your Muscles

Work your way through your body's various muscle groups, one at a time:

- Start with your feet first. Pay attention to the soles of your feet, sense any strain there, and then give them a conscious mental command to completely relax.

- Proceed to your calf muscles and your lower legs and then thighs. Give every muscle group the same attention and instruct them to unwind one after the other.

- Proceed to work on your buttocks and abdomen. If it helps you concentrate more on the muscles, you can tense and relax each muscle group in turn.

- Work your way up through the muscles in your chest, arms, shoulders, neck, face, and scalp. Do not forget to pay attention to, and relax, your tongue.

As you progressively relax your muscle groups, you should feel your body sink further into the mattress or chair when you are correctly performing PMR.

Keep your Breath Awareness

As you release each muscle group, also focus on your breathing. Inhale as you focus on your muscle group and exhale as you relax them. Breathe deeply and rhythmically.

Concentrate on Body Sensations

Pay attention to the tension and relaxation sensations as you contract and release each muscle group. Take note of how the muscles relax and release tension.

Repeat as Necessary

Repeat this exercise daily if you can. Once the muscle groups are finished, pause for a short while to experience a general sense of well-being throughout your body. You should finish each session with full body relaxation.

Remember that at first, your mind may be racing so fast that it will be hard for you to concentrate or lie still. Don't give up; instead, pause the exercise and pick it up later when you are feeling a bit more at ease.

Efficient use of PMR requires a commitment to consistent practise. You may utilise it as part of your regular regimen or if you're feeling tense or nervous. It can be applied alone or in conjunction with other relaxation or stress-reduction techniques. You may also do PMR by following along with online guided recordings or apps if you find it difficult to practise on your own.

Tensing Your Solar Plexus Muscles

One old and well-practiced technique to help actors or public speakers, is to tense your solar plexus muscles several times right before you get up to speak or perform. The solar plexus is located where the lowest point of your sternum (the bone located in the middle of your chest), and the uppermost portion of your abdomen, intersect. To apply this method, simply put your finger on the area and press inward while tensing the muscles of the solar plexus to resist. This manoeuvre prevents the release of noradrenalin and adrenalin from your adrenal glands.

Overcoming Fear and Panic Attacks

Techniques for Grounding

When panic unsettles your thoughts, you need a process to help you return to equilibrium. To do this concentrate on your local surroundings. Describe, touch, or count the items in your immediate environment. Concentrating on your surroundings helps you return to the present and regain focus.

Positive Self-Talk

Use logical, upbeat language to refute and question negative ideas. Swap out catastrophic thinking with more sensible viewpoints.

Mindfulness

One may cultivate a state of mindfulness by the implementation of various protocols, so enabling a reduction in anxiety levels and an increased ability to remain grounded in the present moment. For instance, individuals acquire the ability to critically analyse their ideas and emotions without engaging in evaluative assessments. Instead of categorising ideas as "positive" or "negative," one acknowledges them without assigning any evaluative judgement.

This practise aids in mitigating self-criticism and self-judgment. Mindfulness facilitates the cultivation of acceptance towards any mental or physical phenomena that may emerge. Instead of attempting to alter or evade unpleasant emotions or ideas, individuals acquire the ability to embrace them and examine them with a sense of curiosity and receptiveness.

Mindful communication entails the practise of being completely engaged and focused throughout interpersonal exchanges. Active listening refers to the practise of attentively receiving information without promptly constructing a reply, while concurrently maintaining an awareness of one's own emotional state and reactions during interpersonal exchanges. These techniques, along with other ones, can be incorporated into one's daily routine to foster heightened self-awareness, mitigate stress levels, and augment general well-being.

Cognitive-Behavioural Therapy (CBT)

(CBT) is an extensively used, empirically supported psychotherapy that focuses on the connection between ideas, feelings, and actions. It is predicated on the notion that our ideas and perceptions of the world, other people, and ourselves have a profound impact on our feelings and behaviours. CBT was created in the 1960s by Aaron T. Beck and Albert Ellis, and it has since grown to be one of the most popular and successful therapy modalities for a variety of mental health conditions. You will see that it is referred to quite frequently in this book.

The following is a brief overview of the ideas and elements of CBT:

Cognitive Restructuring

Cognitive behavioural therapy (CBT) starts with the identification and correction of illogical or maladaptive thought processes, often known as cognitive distortions. Among these distortions are catastrophe thinking or outlook, overgeneralising, personalising, and all-or-nothing thinking. The intention is to swap out skewed ideas for more sensible, realistic ones.

Behavioural Techniques

CBT incorporates behavioural tactics to target maladaptive

Overcoming Fear and Panic Attacks

behaviours and strengthen adaptive ones. This might entail creating coping mechanisms, defining clear objectives, and segmenting challenging jobs into do-able chunks.

Homework

To help clients practise and apply the skills they have learnt in therapy to real-world circumstances, homework assignments are frequently assigned to them. This encourages the use of therapeutic strategies in everyday life and active learning.

Exposure

Cognitive behavioural therapy frequently uses exposure procedures in the treatment of anxiety disorders, such as phobias and post-traumatic stress disorder (PTSD). Through incremental exposure to feared stimuli, memories, or circumstances, exposure therapy helps patients face and conquer their fears.

Self-Monitoring

In between therapy sessions, clients are urged to keep an eye on their feelings, ideas, and actions. Self-monitoring aids in the therapeutic process by enabling people to recognise trends and triggers.

Viewpoint

Cognitive Behavioural Therapy acknowledges the influence of ingrained ideas, or conceptual frameworks, about self and the outside environment, and their effect on the development of cognitive distortions. In CBT, examining and changing these fundamental beliefs is a crucial component.

Empirical Approach

Cognitive Behavioural Therapy is guided by an empirical approach, which means that its techniques and interventions are based on facts and scientific evidence. To guarantee its efficacy, it is updated and investigated often.

Time-Limited and Goal-Oriented

CBT is commonly regarded as a focused, time-limited therapy. Together, clients and therapists set goals over the course of therapy and track advancement.

Collaborative Approach

CBT is applied in an involved and collaborative way. Patients should be encouraged to play an active role in treatment, challenge existing views, and try out novel approaches to thinking and acting.

Application

Cognitive behavioural therapy is incredibly flexible and may be used to treat a variety of mental health issues, such as eating disorders, anxiety disorders, depression, OCD, and post-traumatic stress disorder (PTSD).

Empowerment

Cognitive behavioural therapy gives people the tools they need to better handle their emotional health and deal with life's obstacles.

Cognitive Behavioural Therapy (CBT) is the gold standard for treating a wide range of psychiatric conditions since it has been shown to be successful in several clinical trials. Because of its methodical and systematic approach, it is a useful option for anyone looking to acquire skills and techniques to deal with their psychological concerns. It is also accessible to a wide range of individuals since it may be utilised in self-help forms, group therapy, and individual treatment.

More Notes on Exposure Therapy

As a treatment approach exposure therapy is used to treat anxiety disorders, including phobias, obsessive-compulsive disorder (OCD), post-traumatic stress disorder (PTSD), and other problems marked by excessive fear and avoidance practises. The main objective of exposure therapy is to assist patients in facing their fears and progressively desensitising them to the circumstance, object, or idea that they are afraid of. This will help them feel less anxious and stop engaging in avoidance activities.

Here are some essential ideas and the way exposure treatment operates:

Evaluation

To identify the person's unique anxieties, triggers, and avoidance habits, the therapist starts by doing a comprehensive evaluation. The correct exposure targets are identified in part by this evaluation.

Development of an Apprehension Hierarchy

The client and therapist work together to develop an exposure hierarchy based on the evaluation. The scenarios, items, or events linked to the phobia are listed in this hierarchy in order of least to most, anxiety-provoking. This hierarchy functions as an exposure exercise road map.

Exposure

The mainstay of the therapy is exposure. This is carried out by introducing the least anxiety-provoking item in the anxiety hierarchy to the patients first and then progressively exposing them to more anxiety-provoking stimuli.

Exposure can occur in several ways:

Real Exposure

Being gradually exposed in real life to items or circumstances that cause dread. For instance, a person who is afraid of flying can begin by going to the airport but not getting on an aircraft.

Imaginary Exposure

The client discusses and vividly imagines the situation that causes them anxiety. This is frequently applied to PTSD therapy.

Virtual Reality (VR) Exposure

Using virtual reality technology, controlled situations that are realistic may sometimes be created for exposure treatment.

Response Prevention (for OCD)

Response prevention is frequently used for treating OCD. This entails stifling the want to perform obsessive routines or avoidance behaviours after being exposed to a known stimulus or trigger.

Extended and Repetitive Exposure

Usually, the client is exposed in a controlled way to the anxiety-inducing circumstance several times, and they stay there long enough for the anxiety to pass (habituation).

Overcoming Fear and Panic Attacks

Gradually the brain comes to understand that the feared consequence or outcome does not materialise from the exposure, the associated anxiety gradually diminishes.

Using a well-planned anxiety hierarchy guarantees that exposure begins with situations that are controllable and cause less anxiety before moving on to more difficult ones.

Consent and Collaboration

The client and the therapist work together to deliver exposure treatment, and permission is required at every stage. The person in question participates actively in the choice-making process.

Controlled Exposure

Under strict supervision of a qualified therapist, exposure is carried out in a safe and regulated setting. This guarantees the client's security and welfare all along the way.

Graded Exposure

Gradual exposure helps the person gain confidence and adjust to progressively higher anxiety levels.

Homework Assignments

To reinforce progress, clients are frequently given exposure tasks to practise in between therapy sessions.

In summary

The aim of exposure treatment is to help patients sustain their therapeutic progress by applying their newly acquired knowledge to everyday circumstances.

The foundation of exposure treatment is the idea of classical conditioning and habituation. It assists people in rewiring their brain's reaction to frightening stimuli, which eventually lowers anxiety and avoidance habits. Although exposure therapy can be difficult and will cause anxiety, it is a very successful treatment that can significantly enhance a person's quality of life. The process is usually carried out by qualified mental health specialists who compassionately and expertly lead individuals through it.

Management and Medication

To assist control panic episodes, a doctor or psychiatrist may occasionally prescribe medication. Reducing the frequency and intensity of panic attacks can be accomplished with antidepressants and anti-anxiety drugs (see more later).

Lifestyle Modifications

Prioritise sleep, consume a balanced diet, and engage in regular exercise to maintain a healthy lifestyle. These routines can aid in lowering anxiety and tension. Cut back on your use of stimulants like caffeine, cigarettes, and other substances that might make you more anxious or cause panic episodes.

Time management

To avoid feeling overburdened, arrange and rank your duties and/or studies. It might help make projects feel less overwhelming to break them down into smaller, more manageable phases.

Support System

Talk to dependable family members about your experiences so they can provide emotional support. Discussing your

Overcoming Fear and Panic Attacks

emotions with someone non-judgemental that you trust will reduce anxiety.

Self-Care

Take part in self-care activities that encourage calmness and wellbeing, including yoga or enjoyable pastimes. Try to keep a light-hearted attitude and look for chances to laugh. Laughing naturally elevates one's mood.

Self-compassion

You may show yourself compassion by being kind and understanding to yourself - stop being your harshest critic, especially when things are tough.

Keep a Panic Diary

Recording your panic episodes in a journal can assist in identifying trends, causes, and aggravating circumstances. When planning a course of therapy, your healthcare professional may benefit from this documented knowledge.

Also, in the diary create an emergency plan that outlines what to do in the event of a panic attack. This might include practising relaxation methods, having a reliable friend or family member you can contact, or knowing when to seek emergency medical assistance if you have worries about your physical health.

Be aware that absorbing what works best for you may need some trial and error when it comes to handling panic attacks. If your panic attacks are severely interfering with your life or if you are finding it difficult to control them on your own, get expert assistance. The frequency and severity of panic attacks may be effectively controlled by individuals armed with appropriate methods and guidance.

An Overview of Prescription Medicines

Panic disorder and other kinds of anxiety disorders are treated with a variety of pharmaceutical drugs. It is crucial to remember that medicine needs to be furnished and administered by a qualified healthcare professional, usually a primary care physician or a psychiatrist. The exact type and degree of the anxiety condition, as well as the individual's particular situation, will determine which prescription is best.

The following are some medications that are frequently recommended to treat anxiety and panic:

Selective Serotonin Re-uptake Inhibitors

Examples of selective serotonin re-uptake inhibitors (SSRIs) are paroxetine (Paxil), escitalopram (Lexapro), sertraline (Zoloft), and fluoxetine (Prozac). For several anxiety disorders, such as panic disorder and generalised anxiety disorder, SSRIs are frequently recommended as the initial course of treatment. They function by raising serotonin levels in the brain, which aids with mood and anxiety regulation.

Serotonin-Norepinephrine Re-uptake Inhibitors

Examples of serotonin-noradrenaline re-uptake inhibitors (SNRIs) are duloxetine (Cymbalta) and venlafaxine (Effexor). SNRIs are used to treat a variety of anxiety disorders by raising serotonin and noradrenaline levels in the brain.

Benzodiazepines

Alprazolam (Xanax), lorazepam (Ativan), diazepam (Valium), and clonazepam (Klonopin) are a few examples of benzodiazepines. Fast-acting drugs, benzodiazepines can relieve anxiety symptoms quickly, but because they carry a risk of dependency and withdrawal, they are usually only taken temporarily. They function by amplifying the natural calming effects of the neurotransmitter GABA.

Buspirone

Buspirone, often known as Buspar, is an anti-anxiety drug that is less sedative and less likely to cause dependency than benzodiazepines. Although it can be used for other anxiety disorders as well, it is frequently given for generalised anxiety disorder.

Beta-Blockers

Examples of beta-blockers are indral (propranolol) and tenormin (atenolol). Although they are rarely given as first-line therapies for anxiety disorders, beta-blockers may be employed to tackle certain symptoms, such as tremors and a fast heartbeat linked to situational or performance anxieties.

Tricyclic antidepressants (TCAs)

Tofranil (imipramine) and Anafranil (clomipramine) are examples of TCAs. They are older antidepressants but are occasionally utilised as substitutes to less effective or poorly tolerated medicinal products. Compared with SSRIs and SNRIs, they have higher adverse side effects.

Monoamine Oxidase Inhibitors (MAOIs)

Nardil (phenelzine) and Parnate (tranylcypromine) are good examples. Due to dietary and pharmaceutical interaction limitations, MAOIs are usually only used for anxiety disorders that are resistant to other treatments.

IMPORTANT NOTE
Tricyclic antidepressants and Monoamine Oxidase Inhibitors must never be combined together as they can cause serotonin toxicity/syndrome which is potentially fatal.

Anticonvulsant Medicines

Pregabalin (Lyrica) and gabapentin (Neurontin) are two examples of anticonvulsant drugs that may be used to treat anxiety disorders.

Only a healthcare professional ought to determine the medication, its dosage, and duration of therapy after conducting a comprehensive assessment of the patient's needs and condition. Individuals receiving medication for anxiety disorders should be monitored and be well informed about the possible dangers of the medications by their healthcare professional.

The most effective method for treating anxiety is frequently a mix of medicine and psychotherapy.

Complementary and Alternative Therapies

Often referred to as complementary and alternative medicine (CAM), alternative and complementary therapies cover a broad spectrum of methods and techniques that may not be part of traditional Western medicine. These therapies are applied to enhance health and well-being in addition to or, in few cases, instead of traditional medical treatments. While many complementary and alternative medicine (CAM) therapies have been shown to be beneficial, others may pose hazards and lack scientific backing so should only be taken up after the recommendation of your treatment team.

The following are a few typical complementary and alternative therapies:

Overcoming Fear and Panic Attacks

Meditation

Meditation is a mind-body technique used to train attention and awareness, develop mental clarity, and encourage relaxation. It includes focusing the mind on a specific object, idea, or action. It is an age-old practise with origins in many spiritual and cultural traditions (because of its many psychological, emotional, and physical advantages). It has become quite popular in today's world.
While there are many different types of meditation, each with its own special methods and aims, they all aim to achieve inner peace and calm the mind.

Here are a few essential elements of meditation.

Guided Meditation

In guided meditation, you sit through a recorded meditation that is conducted by a teacher. These meditations frequently centre on certain topics, such self-improvement, stress relief, or relaxation. They are most useful for beginners and first timers.

Centred Meditation

Buddhism is the source of mindfulness meditation, which places a strong focus on paying attention to the present moment without passing judgement. Practitioners build mindfulness and acceptance of whatever happens in their experience by focusing on their breath, thoughts, body sensations, or external stimuli.

Transcendental Meditation (TM)

Using a word or phrase (mantra) that is silently repeated to calm the mind and achieve a state of peaceful awareness, TM as a mantra meditation is renowned for being straightforward and simple to use.

Warm-heartedness Metta Meditation

Entails cultivating love, compassion, and kindness for both oneself and other people. To generate good feelings, practitioners usually repeat words or affirmations.

Tai Chi and Yoga

Covered in more detail elsewhere, these movement-based techniques use meditation as a fundamental element. While Tai Chi places more focus on slow, flowing motions and intense concentration, yoga meditation incorporates synchronised breath and movement.

Advantages of Meditation

One of the most debilitating problems of being very nervous is not being able to quiet one's thoughts. You can't focus because your mind is racing in all directions. Attempting to read a book while experiencing anxiety becomes a near impossible task. What happens is that the same page is read and re-read repeatedly without the reader completely absorbing the material.

The goal of meditation is to help you focus your thoughts so precisely that you can quiet your mind and have comprehensive control over your thoughts. By increasing relaxation, soothing the nervous system, and lowering the production of stress hormones, meditation can help reduce stress levels.

People who meditate can better control their emotions and become more conscious of them. Through self-reflection and insight, meditation fosters a deeper awareness of oneself and one's cognitive functions.

Overcoming Fear and Panic Attacks

By relaxing the mind and lowering rumination at night, meditation can also lessen insomnia as well as enhance the quality of sleep that is obtained.
Consistent meditation practise can help cultivate a more balanced and adaptive mentality thus increasing the capacity to overcome life's obstacles.

Practicing Meditation

When seeking focus and relaxation the theme should be set by now:

Choose a quiet space. Select a comfortable, peaceful area where you won't be bothered.

Choose a Comfortable Position. You can meditate while lying down or sitting on a chair, cushion, or the floor. Maintain a calm and straight spine.

Decide how long you want to meditate. Set a time limit. Beginners might begin with a short period and progressively extend it.

Concentrate Your Attention. Decide on a meditation method and focal point, such your breathing, a mantra, or a particular imagery.

Breathe Naturally. Let your breath come to you naturally, and don't attempt to force it. Instead, notice and study it closely.

Be Patient. During meditation, it is common for the mind to wander. When it occurs, return your attention to your selected meditation object in a kind and non-judgmental manner. After the allotted time for your meditation, take a few deep breaths and return your attention gradually to the present moment.

Practise Often. To fully benefit from meditation, consistency is essential. Create a regular meditation schedule that suits you.

Since meditation is a personal practise, there is no one method that works best for everyone. It is advisable to experiment with several meditation techniques and choose the one that most suits your needs. Whether your goals are to overcome panic attacks, improve attention span, reduce stress, relax, or grow spiritually, meditation may be a useful technique for fostering mental and emotional health.

I truly cannot recommend the practice of meditation strong enough.

Acupuncture

In acupuncture, tiny needles are inserted into predetermined body sites as part of a traditional Chinese medicine procedure based on the idea of balancing Qi, pronounced "chee", or life energy, and travels along channels called meridians. Since ancient times, acupuncture has been used to treat a variety of illnesses relating to the body, mind, and spirit.

While it is widely used for pain control, sometimes people use acupuncture in addition to other therapies to help control their anxiety. Some people find acupuncture to be a soothing and helpful supplement to their anxiety management plan, even if it may not be a main or stand-alone treatment for severe anxiety problems.

Here are some ways that acupuncture could help with anxiety:

Overcoming Fear and Panic Attacks

Reduction of Stress

Many patients report feeling calmer and less stressed after receiving acupuncture treatment, since the sessions are frequently soothing. Even just the act of lying down in a calm place focussing on your sensations while having acupuncture can help induce relaxation.

Neurotransmitter Modulation

Acupuncture may have an impact on the brain's neurotransmitters, which include noradrenaline and serotonin which are involved in mood control. The symptoms of anxiety may be lessened by acupuncture through influencing these neurotransmitters.

Nervous System Regulation

Acupuncture has the potential to affect the autonomic nervous system, which may assist in maintaining a balance between the sympathetic "fight or flight" reaction and the parasympathetic "rest and digest" response. This equilibrium may help people feel less anxious.

Diminished Physical signs

Tension in the muscles, headaches, and digestive problems are common physical signs of anxiety. These bodily problems may be lessened with acupuncture, improving general wellbeing.

Better Sleep

Those who suffer from anxiety frequently have trouble falling asleep. Acupuncture may help improve the quality of sleep, which can lessen anxiety during the day.

Holistic Approach

Acupuncture is frequently administered in a holistic manner, considering the patient's general health as well as any possible underlying reasons of their anxiety in addition to treating anxiety symptoms.

Vital Things to consider:

Individual Response. Acupuncture's ability to relieve anxiety varies from patient to patient. While some people might not benefit very much, others could find considerable relief. To make sure acupuncture is in line with your treatment plan, it is imperative that you talk to your mental health practitioner about your intension to use it.

Licenced Practitioners. It is important to select a licenced, experienced acupuncturist who follows safety and hygiene regulations.

Regularity. It frequently takes many treatments for acupuncture to provide observable results. Discuss the suggested course of therapy with your acupuncturist.

Communication. To make sure that your treatments are coordinated and that any changes in your symptoms or general well-being are tracked, keep lines of communication open with your healthcare team, which includes your acupuncturist and mental health physician.

It is important to undertake acupuncture with an open mind, reasonable expectations, and after consulting with licenced healthcare experts, just as with any supplementary therapy.

Overcoming Fear and Panic Attacks

Herbal Medicine

Throughout the ages, people have utilised herbal medicines, also referred to as herbal remedies or botanical supplements, to treat a variety of health issues, including anxiety. Certain herbs have demonstrated potential in lowering anxiety symptoms. However herbal therapies should not be used in place of evidence-based treatments for anxiety disorders, such as psychotherapy or pharmaceuticals.

It is crucial to remember that everyone's experience with herbal treatments varies, so speak with a healthcare professional before using them, particularly if you have underlying medical concerns or are currently taking medication.

The following plants are frequently used to treat anxiety:

Lavender (Lavandula angustifolia)

The sedative and relaxing qualities of lavender are widely recognised. It can be taken as an herbal supplement in the form of capsules or teas; also, it is frequently used as an essential oil in aromatherapy. According to certain research, lavender may help lessen mild to moderate anxiety.

Passionflower (Passiflora incarnata)

In the past, people have used passionflower to cure anxiety and sleeplessness. Studies indicate that it might have a relaxing impact and aid in lessening the symptoms of anxiety. It comes in a variety of forms, such as teas and capsules.

Valerian (Valeriana officinalis)

The herb Valerian is also frequently used to enhance relaxation and sleep quality. It can be found in herbal drinks or as a supplement. Valerian may lessen anxiety and enhance the quality of sleep.

Kava (Piper methysticum)

The native South Pacific plant kava is prized for its sedative and relaxing properties. It has been applied to reduce tension and anxiety. However, there have been worries about possible liver damage linked to kava consumption, and there is still disagreement over its safety.

Chamomile (Matricaria chamomilla)

Chamomile is a mild plant that is frequently used to ease anxiety and encourage calmness. It is usually taken as tea. Although there is little data on chamomile's ability to reduce anxiety, it is usually regarded as harmless.

Ashwagandha (Withania somnifera)

Ashwagandha, is an adaptogenic plant that is used in Ayurvedic medicine to lessen anxiety and stress. According to some research, it could help reduce the levels of stress hormones and enhance general wellbeing.

Rhodiola (Rhodiola rosea)

Another adaptogenic herb that has been researched for its ability to lessen stress and anxiety is rhodiola. It is said to lessen anxiety symptoms and lift your spirits.

Ginkgo Biloba

Although studies have focused on the possible cognitive advantages of ginkgo biloba, there is also evidence that the herb may have modest anxiolytic (anxiety-reducing) properties.

Use caution and speak with a healthcare professional before beginning any natural remedy for anxiety. You ought to be mindful about any interactions with any prescription medications you may be taking, allergies, and the herb's general safety.

Furthermore, there is variation in the efficacy of herbal medicines, and it might take some time to ascertain whether a specific plant is beneficial for your anxiety symptoms. When contemplating herbal supplements, always select trustworthy brands and be aware of any negative side effects. It is highly advised that those with severe or persistent anxiety problems seek the advice of a mental health professional for evidence-based therapy.

Aromatherapy

Aromatherapy is a holistic medical technique that enhances mental, emotional, and physical health by using the fragrances and odours of essential oils made from different plants. It is frequently used as an adjunctive treatment to lower stress and anxiety levels and elevate mood.

Here are some ways that aromatherapy helps reduce anxiety:

Soothing and Relaxation

Calming and relaxing qualities are shared by many essential oils, which can aid in reducing tension and anxiety by soothing the nervous system.

Mood Enhancement

The limbic system, which controls emotions and memories, is the mechanism through which aromatherapy affects mood. Some fragrances have the power to elevate and enhance mood, which may lessen depressive and anxious sensations.

Stress Reduction

Breathing in pleasant fragrances can cause the body to release endorphins, which are naturally occurring narcotic mood enhancers, and lower levels of stress chemicals like cortisol.

Sleep Enhancement

Since insomnia is frequently associated with anxiety, aromatherapy can help manage insomnia and enhance the quality of sleep.

Supportive Action

Meditation and deep breathing exercises are examples of mindfulness and relaxation techniques. By adding aromatherapy to these techniques, you can increase their potency in lowering anxiety.

Typical Essential Oils for Nervousness

Lavender

The relaxing and soothing effects of lavender essential oil are widely recognised. It is frequently used to encourage relaxation, lessen anxiety, and enhance the quality of sleep.

Chamomile

German and Roman chamomile essential oils are both utilised for their sedative properties. They may lessen the signs of worry and tension.

Bergamot

Known for its zesty and energising aroma, bergamot essential oil is frequently used to treat anxiety and depression symptoms.

Overcoming Fear and Panic Attacks

Frankincense

Grounding and centring qualities of Frankincense essential oil are well-known, and they can aid in lowering tension and anxiety levels.

Ylang-Ylang

Ylang-ylang essential oil is used to ease stress and encourage relaxation. It has a pleasant, flowery aroma.

Rose

Rose essential oil is linked to emotions of consolation and emotional reinforcement. It can be used to improve mood and lessen anxiety.

Applying Aromatherapy to Treat Anxiety

Diffusion

Using an essential oil diffuser is one of the most popular techniques. You may inhale the aroma of essential oils throughout the day or while using relaxation techniques thanks to this device, which releases their perfume into the atmosphere.

Topical Application

The skin can be treated with diluted essential oils, usually on pulse points such as the neck and wrists. Before applying essential oil to the skin, make sure you dilute it with a carrier oil such as Grapeseed, Avocado or Jojoba oils.

Breathing In

You may either inhale the scent straight from the container or by dabbing a few drops onto a cotton ball or tissue. To experience the relaxing benefits, inhale slowly and deeply.

Bathing

A warm bath enhanced with a few drops of essential oil may be calming and relaxing.

Massage Adjuvant

During a massage, diluted essential oils are used in aromatherapy to encourage relaxation and ease stress.

Aromatherapy is not a stand-alone treatment for severe anxiety disorders, but it can be a useful tool for controlling anxiety. A patch test or consultation with a healthcare expert is advised prior to using essential oils, as some people may have allergies/sensitivities.

Massage Therapy

Massage therapy is a well-liked and successful supplementary method for lowering anxiety and encouraging relaxation. By manually manipulating the body's soft tissues and muscles it releases and dissipates stress.

The following are some ways that massage therapy might help with anxiety:

Tension Reduction

Anxiety is frequently linked to tight and tense muscles, which can be relieved with a massage. The capacity of massage treatment to promote relaxation and lessen muscle tension is well-known. Massage also lowers the stress hormone cortisol, and the physical manipulation and pressure used, further encourages the release of feel-good chemicals like dopamine and serotonin.

Overcoming Fear and Panic Attacks

Sleep Enhancement

Anxiety can cause problems with the quality of your sleep. By calming the body and mind, massage therapy can help people sleep better by facilitating a more effortless transition from being awake to sleeping.

Improved Mood

The feeling of calm and well-being that comes from getting a massage both during and after can lift your spirits and lessen the feelings of sadness and anxiety.

Mind-Body Connection

By helping people become more conscious of their bodies and feelings, massage therapy helps people enhance a stronger mind-body connection that can lower anxiety and increase mindfulness.

Endorphin Release

Endorphins are naturally occurring sedatives and mood enhancers that can be released during massage therapy. This can support relaxation and a general sense of well-being.

Reduced Heart Rate and Blood Pressure

Research has demonstrated that massage treatment helps lower blood pressure and heart rate, frequently high in those who suffer from anxiety.

Enhanced Body Awareness

Receiving a massage can help people become more aware of their bodies and the present moment, which can help calm racing thoughts and anxieties.

Massage Techniques

Swedish massage
Long, flowing strokes are used in this mild form of massage to ease muscular tension and encourage relaxation.

Deep Tissue Massage
This type of massage works on the connective tissue and muscle at deeper levels. It may be too strong for some people, but it can be helpful for those with persistent muscular tightness.

Aromatherapy Massage
As mentioned earlier, to improve mood and relaxation, aromatherapy massage uses essential oils. There are several essential oils that are recognised to be relaxing.

Hot Stone Massage
This type of massage uses warm stones applied to the body to ease tense muscles. It can be calming and more relaxing for muscles to be heated in this way.

Thai Massage
Thai massage is very useful to relieve stress and at the same time increase flexibility, as it incorporates acupressure with aided stretching and yoga-style movements.

Reflexology
Reflexology is the study and manipulation of certain pressure points in the soles of the feet that are understood to represent different bodily systems and organs. It can greatly ease

tension and encourage relaxation. Particularly in those heavier individuals, or those who spend long periods of the day on their feet

When considering massage therapy for anxiety, it is wise to speak with a certified and experienced massage therapist. They can adjust the pressure and methods of the massage to your individual needs.

Massage therapy is frequently used as a complimentary therapy in addition to other therapies, such as counselling or medication in dealing with anxiety problems. Make sure massage therapy is in line with your entire treatment plan by keeping in constant contact with your healthcare team.

Mindfulness

The psychological and meditation practise of mindfulness entails focusing on the present moment with attention that is non-judgemental. It is frequently employed as a therapeutic method to address emotional and mental health issues including anxiety. The efficacy of mindfulness-based interventions in lowering anxiety symptoms has led to the rise in popularity of programmes like Mindfulness-Based Stress Reduction (MBSR) and Mindfulness-Based Cognitive Therapy (MBCT).

Here are some ways that mindfulness might help with anxiety:

Thought Pattern Recognition

Mindfulness enables people to observe their thoughts objectively giving greater awareness of their thinking patterns. People benefit from this by being more conscious of the narratives they carry about their anxieties and fears.

Avoid Over Thinking

Individuals who suffer from anxiety frequently ruminate, returning again and again to the same upsetting ideas or situations. Rumination may be stopped by practising mindfulness, which focuses attention on the here and now thus allowing you to leave past events behind.

Stress Reduction

The body's stress reaction is countered by the relaxation response which is triggered by mindfulness techniques like meditation and deep breathing. As a result, this relaxation in turn calms the mind.

Emotional Regulation

Mindfulness training makes people more aware of their emotions, which enables them to react to unpleasant feelings with better self-compassion and clarity. This will lessen anxiety and feelings of dread generated by such thoughts.

Concentration Enhancement and Focus

Mindfulness exercises on a regular basis can improve focus and cognitive control. This can be especially beneficial for patients when they experience trouble focusing because of tension and stress.

Acceptance and Non-Judgment

Being mindful helps recognise one's feelings, especially anxiety, without passing judgement. The emotional burden and reluctance that come with worry might be lessened by accepting it without passing judgement.

Overcoming Fear and Panic Attacks

Coping Strategies

Mindfulness offers people useful techniques for reducing tension, such as mindful body scans and movement, and deep breathing exercises. In time these will be incorporated in your efforts to overcome and dominate the condition.

Keeping Your Focus on the Here and Now

Doubts or fears about the future are common causes of anxiety. By keeping people anchored in the present, mindfulness allows them to control their worry impulses.

How to Practice Mindfulness

Breathe Mindfully

As previously described, observe how your breath enters and exits your body. Allow yourself to effortlessly be fully present in each breath.

Mindful Body Scans

Examine and sense your whole body from head to toe, focusing on any tense or uncomfortable spots. Inhale deeply and mentally order the tense areas to relax.

Walking with Awareness

Pay close attention to every stride you take and the feeling of your feet hitting the ground. Take note of your surroundings sights, sounds and sensations.

Eat Mindfully

By taking your time and enjoying every mouthful of your food. Take note of the food's flavour, texture, and aroma.

This practice can also be utilised in weight control programs.

Journal Mindfully

Express your ideas and emotions in writing, free from criticism. You can learn more about your thought patterns and anxiety triggers by doing this.

Spend some time doing mindfulness meditation every day. It just takes a few focussed minutes. Locate a peaceful area, take a comfortable seat, and concentrate on your breathing or a different focal point. In addition, engage in mindful movement exercises that integrate physical activity and mindfulness such as yoga, tai chi, or qigong.

While mindfulness may be very helpful in lowering anxiety, it might not offer relief right away, and its advantages can become more obvious with continued practise. Alongside other evidence-based therapies like cognitive-behavioural therapy (CBT) or medication, mindfulness can be utilised as a supplemental therapy for those with severe anxiety or anxiety disorders.

Homeopathy

The field of homoeopathy is part of complementary and alternative medicine (CAM). It is founded on the ideas of "like-cures-like", and where very diluted natural substances, which would in larger amounts, otherwise produce the same symptoms of the ailment itself, will encourage the body's natural healing processes to take hold.

Although some people use homoeopathy as a treatment for a variety of health issues, including anxiety. It is vital to remember that there is little scientific proof of the efficacy of homeopathic remedies, and the matter is still up for

Overcoming Fear and Panic Attacks

discussion among medical professionals.

Here are some important things to think about in relation to anxiety and homoeopathy:

Individualised Care

Homeopathic doctors frequently recommend treatments based on each patient's particular set of physical, emotional, and mental symptoms. A distinguishing feature of homoeopathy is its customised approach.

Extremely Diluted Constituents

Homeopathic medicines are made by vigorously shaking an ingredient (typically derived from a plant, mineral, or animal source) after it has been diluted several times. The resultant solutions are very diluted, sometimes to the point where the original substance's molecules are completely gone.

According to homoeopathy, these extremely diluted medications nevertheless have a "memory" of the original ingredient and can encourage the body's natural healing process.

Important Note

According to several systematic reviews and meta-analyses, many in the scientific community state that there is insufficient empirical data to demonstrate the effectiveness of homoeopathy. They contend that there is no clearly discernible difference between homoeopathic treatments and placebos for treating a variety of conditions, including anxiety.

They contend that homoeopathic remedies have the potential to alleviate symptoms for certain people strictly because of the placebo effect. The effect is a recognised medical phenomenon in which apparent improvements in health result solely from treatment expectations. Since homeopathic treatments are greatly diluted and contain very little of the original substance, they are typically regarded as safe when taken as advised by a trained practitioner.

It is crucial to speak with a certified homeopathic practitioner as there are differences in the safety of certain specific medicines or preparations. If you are thinking about homeopathic treatment for anxiety or any other health issue, you should speak with a licenced healthcare professional, ideally one who practises both conventional and alternative medicine,

In the end, choosing to utilise homoeopathy for anxiety or any other ailment should be decided after consulting with licenced medical experts who can offer advice on evidence-based therapies and the advantages and disadvantages of each. Prioritising therapy with a solid scientific basis is crucial for conditions as serious as anxiety.

Yoga

Yoga is a mind-body discipline that incorporates breathing exercises, relaxation methods, meditation, coupled with physical postures. It has become increasingly popular as an additional strategy for stress and anxiety management.

Regular yoga practise has several potential advantages for anxious people, including:

Stress Reduction

Yoga helps people relax and lessens the stress reaction in their bodies. Deep breathing, meditation, and yoga poses can help reduce cortisol levels, and trigger the relaxation response.

Overcoming Fear and Panic Attacks

Mind-Body Connection

Yoga promotes awareness of the interaction between the mind and body. It can assist people in developing heightened awareness of their emotions and bodily sensations, which can increase their self-awareness and emotional control.

Enhanced Relaxation Skills

Deep breathing exercises and progressive muscular relaxation are two of the relaxation methods that yoga offers to help people handle their anxiety in day-to-day situations.

Benefits for the Body

Consistent yoga practise may enhance balance, flexibility, and physical fitness, all of which can lower stress levels and promote a sense of wellbeing.

Decreased Muscle Tension

Tightness and tension in the muscles are common signs of anxiety. Stretches and postures from yoga can help relieve this tension and lessen the physical discomfort that comes with worry.

Improved Focus and Concentration

Yoga calls for awareness and mental focus. During yoga sessions, mindfulness practises can help people become more focused and concentrated, which can help them manage racing thoughts associated with anxiety.

Improved Sleep

People who suffer from anxiety frequently have insomnia and disturbed sleep. Yoga can enhance both the duration and quality of sleep.

Social Support

Attending yoga lessons in groups may foster a feeling of belonging and social support, both of which are advantageous for people who struggle with anxiety.

Decreased Symptoms

Research has indicated that performing yoga can help reduce anxiety and depressive symptoms. With consistent yoga practise, some people may see notable benefits in their mental health.

It is vital to remember that different people may experience yoga's calming benefits differently. Yoga is frequently used as an adjunctive therapy for people with identified anxiety disorders in addition to evidence-based therapies like medication or cognitive-behavioural therapy.

The following advice may be helpful if you're thinking about using yoga to treat anxiety:

Speak with a Healthcare Professional

See your doctor if you have any physical or medical issues that might interfere with your ability to practise yoga safely.

Select the Correct Style

There are several yoga styles that offer differing degrees of attention and intensity. For the treatment of anxiety, moderate, restorative, and hatha yoga is frequently advised.

Practise frequently

Durability is essential. Over time, consistent yoga practice even for a short while each day can provide more advantages.

Overcoming Fear and Panic Attacks

Practise mindfulness by focusing on the here and now when doing yoga. To further increase the mindfulness component of yoga, pay attention to your breath and your body's feelings.

Seek Guidance

If yoga is new to you, think about enrolling in courses with a certified yoga instructor who can walk you through the correct poses and practises.

Tai Chi

Known by many as Tai Chi Chuan, Tai Chi is an ancient Chinese martial art that has developed into a mind-body exercise that is renowned for its focused, flowing motions. It has grown in popularity as a relaxing workout method that may help with anxiety and stress reduction.

Here are some ways that Tai Chi can help people who are anxious:

Stress Reduction

Tai Chi places a strong focus on deep breathing and slow, deliberate motions, which can aid in triggering the relaxation response and lowering cortisol levels.

Mindfulness

Tai Chi demands a great deal of awareness from its practitioners, who must pay close attention to their breathing, movements, and physical sensations. By encouraging a "Now"-centred awareness that opposes ruminating and worry.

Reduction in muscle tension

Reducing muscular tension and promoting physical relaxation are two benefits of Tai Chi's soft, flowing motions, which can help with the physical symptoms of anxiety.

Enhanced Resilience

Regular Tai Chi practise can improve a person's general stress tolerance, which makes it simpler to handle anxiety triggers and day-to-day obstacles.

Enhanced Balance and Coordination

Tai Chi poses challenges to balance and coordination, which can boost self-esteem and lessen anxiety symptoms for certain people by lowering their fear of falling or losing control. This coupled with the lack of need for high fitness levels make this a very popular practice amongst senior citizens.

Social Interaction

Taking Tai Chi courses may help people feel more connected to others and supported, which is especially helpful for those who struggle with social anxiety.

Breath Control

Deep, conscious breathing exercises are incorporated into Tai Chi, which can help people control their breathing, lessen hyperventilation, and relax their nervous system when they're feeling anxious.

Self-consideration

Practising Tai Chi may be a way to take care of oneself by encouraging self-awareness and self-compassion. This can be beneficial for anxious people who might have trouble with self-criticism.

Cognitive Benefits

According to some studies, Tai Chi may enhance cognitive performance and lessen anxiety-related cognitive disruptions including racing thoughts and difficulties focusing.

Enhance Sleep

The calming effects and effort and exertion related to Tai Chi can improve the quality of your sleep.

Beginning Tai Chi

Locate a Class

Seek Tai Chi courses or seminars in your area that are taught by licenced teachers. Studying Tai Chi with a qualified instructor will help you with its ethos, form, and technique.

Select a Style

There are many different forms of Tai Chi; the most well-known are those are by Yang, Chen, Wu, Hao and Sun. Select a style that best fits your requirements and interests since different styles highlight different facets of the practise.

Practise Often

To reap the full advantages of Tai Chi, consistency is essential. Try to practise daily, even if it is only for short periods.

Combine with Other Strategies

Tai Chi can be a useful addition to your anxiety management toolkit, even if it might not be a stand-alone treatment for severe anxiety disorders. Because of its low-impact, soothing nature, people of all ages and fitness levels may participate in it.

Tai Chi can be utilised in addition to other research-proven anxiety therapies, such as counselling or medication, as a supplemental strategy. Speak with a healthcare professional to find the best course of action for your unique anxiety requirements.

Energy Healing

Using the body's subtle energy systems to create harmony and balance is the goal of energy healing. It is said to be a holistic approach to health. It is crucial to realise that, despite the growing popularity of energy healing techniques like Reiki, acupuncture, and chakra balancing as alternative therapies, there still lacks clear scientific proof to support their efficacy in treating anxiety. The results of energy healing differ from person to person, and it is regarded as a type of complementary and alternative medicine (CAM).

This is a synopsis of energy healing and how it may help with anxiety management:

The fundamental principle of energy healing is that the body possesses an energy system that can be adjusted and regulated to enhance overall health and wellbeing. Energy healing practitioners frequently work with notions like meridians, which are energy routes, chakras, which are energy centres, and the flow of life force energy, known as Prana in India or Qi in China.

Tension Reduction

Overcoming Fear and Panic Attacks

Energy healing sessions are often quite soothing to people, which may help to lower tension and anxiety levels. Energy healing's soothing and centring qualities may aid people in controlling their emotional reactions.

Self-Healing

It is thought that energy healing triggers the body's natural capacity for self-healing. Through the correction of imbalances or blockages in the energy system, it is believed to facilitate the body's inherent healing mechanisms.

Holistic Approach

Energy healing is said to approach health from a holistic perspective, considering not just physical symptoms but also mental, emotional, and spiritual elements. This all-encompassing strategy is in line with the knowledge that anxiety can have a variety of complex origins and outcomes. Deep breathing exercises, meditation, and relaxation techniques are all part of several energy healing therapies, and they may be beneficial in reducing the symptoms of anxiety.

Personal Experience

Energy healing is very personalised when it comes to its efficacy. One person's solution might not be the same for another. After energy healing sessions, some people report feeling a great deal less anxious, while other people might not have the same outcome. There seems to be a close relationship between acceptance level to the approach and its efficacy.

Complementary Approach

Energy healing should be only utilised in addition to more traditional anxiety therapies like psychotherapy or medication. It is not advised to treat anxiety disorders with energy healing on its own.

Safety and Training

It is critical to collaborate with certified, experienced practitioners that follow safety and ethical guidelines while pursuing energy healing. Verify that the practitioner is properly certified or licenced in the field of their modality.

Explore with an Open Mind

If energy healing seems like a good fit for treating your anxiety, think about including it into your overall wellness plan. Have an open mind and be prepared to try out several strategies to see which one suits you the best.

Incorporating energy healing into your anxiety treatment approach necessitates open communication with your healthcare team, including mental health providers. It shouldn't be used in place of evidence-based therapies for moderate/severe or persistent anxiety disorders, even if some people find it to be a useful additional practise for lowering anxiety and encouraging relaxation. Research on the efficacy of energy healing is still in progress, as to its potential application to mental health therapy.

Nutritional Supplements

Vitamins, minerals, and other dietary supplements are occasionally utilised in conjunction with other therapies to treat the symptoms of anxiety. It is crucial to remember that while these supplements could help promote general mental health, they cannot take the place of evidence-based therapies for anxiety disorders, including medicine or psychotherapy. Furthermore, the efficacy of dietary supplements for anxiety varies from person to person, as well as, between individual dietary supplements themselves. Thus, consulting a healthcare professional before using them is strongly advised.

The following is a short list of popular dietary supplements and their possible use in the treatment of anxiety:

Omega-3 Fatty Acids

Rich in anti-inflammatory qualities and are thought to promote better brain function. Omega-3 fatty acids are present in fatty fish (such as salmon and mackerel) and fish oil supplements. According to limited research, taking an omega-3 supplement may help with anxiety symptoms.

Magnesium

Magnesium is a necessary mineral that affects nerve relaxation and function. There is a chance that low magnesium levels exist in certain anxious people. Supplementing with magnesium may help lessen the feelings of anxiety, especially if there is a magnesium deficit in the body.

B vitamins

Some people may exhibit anxiety symptoms if they have low amounts of certain vitamins. There are several B vitamins that are involved in the formation of neurotransmitters which influence mood. These include B6, B9 (folate), and B12. Supplementation might be helpful for people who are deficient.

L-theanine

Green tea contains the amino acid L-theanine. Its ability to induce calmness and lessen anxiety without making people drowsy has been researched.

Probiotics

While research on the relationship between the gastro-intestinal system and the brain has barely got started, but there is evidence that a balanced gut flora may have an impact on anxiety and mood. Supplements containing probiotics may improve gut health, which in turn may benefit mental health.

Herbal supplements

Covered previously.

Adaptogens

Herbs with adaptogenic properties, such as rhodiola and ashwagandha, have been researched for their ability to assist the body adjust to stress and lessen anxiety symptoms. While some people find them useful, additional studies are required to determine their effectiveness.

Cannabidiol substances

Aka CBD is a substance that comes from the cannabis plant and is known to have relaxing and anti-anxiety properties. It comes in several forms, such as oils and capsules. Although CBD has helped some people with their anxiety, it should be considered with caution. Its legality of use differs from country to country. Before considering the use of any product produced from cannabis, verify the rules and regulations in the jurisdiction you find yourself. Please always check and abide by all local laws and regulations.

Important Points to Remember

Overcoming Fear and Panic Attacks

Personal Reaction

The impact of dietary supplements varies between individuals. One person's nutritional solution might not be the same for another. It is critical to exercise caution and speak with a healthcare professional to figure out which supplements are best for you. In any case, there is no doubt that there is great general health benefit in a healthy diet.

Quality and Safety

To guarantee efficacy and safety, select premium supplements from reliable brands. Always abide by the standards and suggested doses.

Speak with a Healthcare Professional

See a certified healthcare professional before beginning any nutritional supplement programme for anxiety, particularly if you use medication, have underlying medical issues, are pregnant, or are breastfeeding a baby.

Approach when Taking Supplements

In addition to evidence-based therapies for anxiety, nutritional supplements are frequently utilised as a supplemental strategy. For severe or persistent anxiety disorders, they shouldn't be used in place of or as the only form of treatment.

It is essential to keep in mind that anxiety management is a customised, intricate process. Comprehensive treatment frequently entails a combination of therapies and lifestyle modifications, such as psychotherapy, medication, regular exercise, stress management strategies and a balanced diet.

Traditional Chinese Medicine (TCM)

Whereas the western scientific and news media has tended to be somewhat dismissive of TCM. It must be acknowledged that as a comprehensive medical approach, traditional Chinese medicine (TCM) has been used for thousands of years in China and other Asian countries and has much inherent merit. TCM includes a wide range of treatments, including as food therapy, acupuncture, herbal medicine, massage (tui na), and movement exercises like Qi Gong and Tai Chi. It takes a holistic approach to health and wellbeing, aiming to harmonise the flow of Yin and Yang energies and Qi, the body's life force (pronounced "chee"). Traditional Chinese Medicine (TCM) has been utilised to treat anxiety and stress, frequently in addition to other medical therapies.

The following are some essential elements of TCM and how they connect to anxiety:

Acupuncture

Covered previously.

Herbal Medicine

Covered previously.

Dietary treatment

The TCM dietary treatment places a strong focus on the value of moderation and balance in food selections. There may be dietary suggestions that are specific to a person depending on their health and constitution. TCM holds that emotional health, especially anxiety, may be impacted by digestive system abnormalities.

Mind-Body Practises

Tai Chi and Qi Gong are two essential TCM movement

Overcoming Fear and Panic Attacks

techniques that are believed to support the development of a strong mind-body connection. These techniques help ease tension, encourage relaxation, and enhance general wellbeing.

Herbal Teas

Covered previously.

Emotional Balance

According to Traditional Chinese Medicine, emotional aspects are vital to general health. Anxiety can be exacerbated by emotional imbalances, such as excessive worry or dread, which can disturb Qi. Practitioners of TCM seek to recognise and correct them.

Constitutional Assessment

To identify the underlying patterns of disharmony that may exacerbate anxiety, TCM practitioners evaluate a person's physical, mental, and emotional constitution.

Customised Care

TCM interventions are extremely personalised, with treatments or cures selected according to the unique disharmony pattern that each patient exhibits. TCM's personalised approach is one of its main characteristics.

It is vital to remember that although many people find TCM treatments beneficial for reducing anxiety, there is little and inconsistent western scientific data to back these claims. This may represent a historical bias which western medicine is guilty of, and more in-depth research is needed.

TCM is frequently used in addition to more traditional

anxiety therapies like psychotherapy or medication. If you're thinking about using TCM to treat your anxiety, speak with a certified practitioner who can offer you a customised evaluation and treatment strategy. To guarantee that every facet of your therapy is well-coordinated and tailored to your individual requirements, always keep lines of communication open with your healthcare team, including mental health specialists.

Holistic Medicine

Holistic medicine is an attitudinal approach to healthcare rather than a particular set of techniques. It presumes to treat the whole person rather than focussing on a specific illness. In order to achieve maximum health and wellbeing, it is said that holistic medicine considers every aspect of a person, including the body, mind, spirit, and emotions. The main goals of holistic medicine are to support the body's own healing processes, encourage balance, and treat the root causes of illnesses. Although holistic methods can be utilised to control anxiety, evidence-based therapies for anxiety disorders should be used in conjunction with them.

The following are some essential elements of holistic medicine and how they relate to anxiety:

Mind-Body Connection

Holistic medicine acknowledges the strong mental-physical link. It underlines how important it is to acknowledge that mental and emotional health have a substantial influence on physical health and vice versa. Since anxiety is a condition having both psychological and physical symptoms, a holistic approach is frequently used to treating it.

One of the best examples of mental-physical linking, can be

Overcoming Fear and Panic Attacks

seen in the work of the late Professor John E. Sarno MD. who was Professor of Rehabilitation Medicine and who championed the theory that pain, in particular back pain, was a symptom of an unconscious distraction from a deeply repressed emotional issue.

In case you suffer from back pain. I highly recommend that you read his book - *Healing back pain: The Mind-Body Connection*.

Nutrition

As noted earlier, a well-balanced diet may affect mood and energy levels and is the cornerstone of general health. Holistic doctors frequently give dietary advice to promote mental health, such as cutting back on sugar, salt and caffeine and eating more nutrient-dense foods.

Movement and Exercise

Research has shown that physical exercise improves mental health. Regular movement and exercise are encouraged by holistic medicine because they can lower stress hormones and induce the production of endorphins, which in turn can relieve anxiety.

Stress Reduction Methods

Mindfulness, progressive muscle relaxation, deep breathing, guided imagery, and meditation are a few examples of stress reduction methods that holistic approaches frequently use. These methods can aid in anxiety management and encourage relaxation.

Herbal Medicine

In holistic medicine, herbal treatments are frequently utilised to treat a variety of health conditions, including anxiety. As mentioned earlier, herbs with relaxing properties, such as passionflower, valerian, and chamomile, are occasionally used as herbal treatments for anxiety.

Holistic treatments

A variety of holistic treatments are used to improve emotional well-being, ease stress, and encourage relaxation. These therapies include acupuncture, massage therapy, aromatherapy, and energy healing (such as Reiki). These techniques are frequently applied in conjunction with other anxiety treatments.

Spiritual and Emotional Well-Being

The significance of spiritual and emotional well-being is recognised by holistic medicine. A feeling of purpose and meaning may be provided by engaging in practises such as mindfulness and meditation, which can benefit people with anxiety by promoting emotional equilibrium.

Individualised Care

A major component of holistic medicine is tailored care for each patient. When creating a treatment plan for anxiety, professionals consider the physical, mental, and emotional requirements of each patient.

Lifestyle Modifications

Adopting holistic methods may include modifying one's way of living to promote general wellbeing. This may entail lowering exposure to pollutants in the environment, developing healthy relationships, and enhancing sleep hygiene.

Integrated Care

Overcoming Fear and Panic Attacks

In addition to traditional anxiety therapies like psychotherapy and medication, holistic medicine can be utilised. To deliver all-encompassing treatment, an integrated method blends the best features of conventional and holistic therapies.

Although many people find using holistic methods to manage their long-term anxiety issues beneficial, it is important to keep in mind that evidence-based therapies for severe anxiety disorders cannot be replaced by holistic medicine.

When seeking holistic treatments for anxiety It is important to speak with licenced professionals who can guide you and make sure the therapies you select fit your unique requirements and situation. To make sure that your treatment plan is well-coordinated and supported by evidence, you should always have open lines of communication with the members of your healthcare team, including the mental health specialists.

It is crucial to use caution while utilising complementary and alternative therapies and to consult with licenced professionals or healthcare providers for advice. While some complementary and alternative medicine (CAM) treatments have shown promise, others are unsupported by research and might not be suitable for all patients or circumstances. Furthermore, it is critical to discuss any CAM therapies you are thinking about with your healthcare team so they can make sure they don't conflict with prescription drugs or other standard treatments. When making healthcare decisions, always give evidence-based medicine priority and seek advice from medical specialists.

You would have noted that when looking into the application of CAM therapies, there exists a common thread on how to handle anxiety and panic. Following some of these common thread approaches can help deliver a long-term solution to the problem.

In summary, the management of panic attacks necessitates a comprehensive and adaptable methodology that requires a holistic and personalised strategy. Throughout this chapter, an examination was conducted on several therapy methods and tactics that provide alleviation, empowerment, and optimism for those grappling with the incapacitating hold of panic attacks.

The previous chapters highlighted the importance of the comprehension of the fundamental origins and stimuli that contribute to the occurrence of panic attacks. Through a comprehensive analysis of the intricate dynamics of genetic, environmental, and psychological elements, both patients and healthcare practitioners are empowered to make well-informed choices on potential courses of therapy. Cognitive-behavioural therapy (CBT) has evolved as a prominent treatment modality, providing clients with the necessary skills to recognise, question, and restructure anxious cognitions and behaviours.

Pharmaceutical interventions, such as the administration of selective serotonin reuptake inhibitors (SSRIs) and benzodiazepines, are crucial in mitigating immediate symptoms and mitigating the likelihood of future panic attack episodes. Nevertheless, it is important to exercise cautious oversight and conduct thorough assessments of their use in order to identify any possible adverse reactions and the likelihood of developing dependency.

The integration of lifestyle adjustments, such as the use of stress reduction strategies, consistent engagement in physical activity, adherence to a well-balanced dietary regimen, and

Overcoming Fear and Panic Attacks

attainment of sufficient sleep, establishes a robust framework for promoting holistic wellness and effectively managing anxiety. In addition, the utilisation of mindfulness and relaxation techniques offers individuals a method to anchor themselves in the current moment, foster resilience, and reduce the anxiety linked to episodes of panic attacks.

The chapter has tried to establish a robust basis for the examination and comprehension of panic episodes, their therapeutic approaches, and the capacity of individuals to endure and overcome challenges. By the integration of information, empathy, and efficacious therapies, it is possible to envision a more promising and harmonious future for those experiencing panic attacks.

CHAPTER 4

THRIVING BEYOND PANIC ATTACKS

Experiencing a panic attack for the first time is trying and upsetting, but many people do learn how to control and get over them. By understanding more about the mechanisms and triggers of anxiety disorders and panic attacks and closely scrutinising their underlying details, they will prove far less intimidating and more rational.

In order to assist in reducing anxiety and calming the nervous system, the practise of regular relaxation techniques through tools like yoga, mindfulness meditation, progressive muscle relaxation, and deep breathing is very effective and strongly recommended. Stress and anxiety are also both decreased by physical activity and physical fitness, so improving your general health, by making regular exercise a part of your weekly schedule should be planned.

Give priority to self-care practises that enhance relaxation and overall health, such as, having a soothing massage once in a while, going on nature walks, or pursuing enjoyable hobbies.

Be aware that while avoiding locations or circumstances that cause panic attacks may help temporarily, doing so usually makes the dread worse. Try to gradually face them to become less sensitive to these triggers over time. Continue seeing your mental health provider on a regular basis even after you've made considerable progress just to make sure you're

Overcoming Fear and Panic Attacks

staying on the correct path and getting helpful supervision moving forward.

Although it will need effort and time, be assured that you will conquer panic episodes and thrive in the process. Keep in mind that every person's path is different, and that improvement happens gradually. Remain dedicated to your treatment plan and acknowledge your accomplishments along the way to full recovery. You will be able to live a life free from the dominance and disruption that panic attacks bring, and you will maintain and enhance your mental and emotional health. All it takes is dedication and the appropriate assistance.

To thrive after experiencing panic attacks, people frequently combine coping mechanisms and lifestyle changes to remove the chance of recurrent episodes and enhance their general wellbeing.

While many have already been mentioned I will reiterate and appraise some here as well.

Lifestyle Modifications

Stress Management

Stress is a state of physical or mental tension caused by a situation the person finds difficult. It can come about from any event or thought that makes you angry, frustrated, or nervous. It can also be seen as the body's reaction to a challenge or demand. Take note that stress can be of benefit if it is in short bursts like when avoiding a dangerous situation. On the other hand, it can be quite detrimental when it is prolonged and persistent.

One of the most important aspects of controlling panic

attacks is lowering stress. Continue including stress-relieving activities like progressive muscle relaxation, yoga, deep breathing exercises, and mindfulness meditation in your everyday routine.

Healthy Diet

Be mindful of what you eat and drink since some food and drink might make anxiety worse. Caffeine, alcohol, and sugary meals should be avoided or limited as they might aggravate anxiety symptoms. Prioritise eating a well-balanced diet that is high in lean proteins, fruits, vegetables, whole grains, and Omega-3 fatty acids, all of which can promote mental health.

Frequent Exercise

Research has indicated that frequent physical activity can lower anxiety and elevate mood. Look for something you can continuously sustain and love doing. On about four days a week, try to get in at least 45 minutes of moderate-intensity exercise that leaves you breathless.

Limit Substance Abuse

Because substances like nicotine, some recreational drugs, and excessive alcohol can exacerbate anxiety symptoms and precipitate panic episodes, it is best to avoid or minimise their usage.

Social Support

Continue to communicate with family and friends. Having social support is crucial for good mental health. Tell someone you can trust about what you've gone through; if necessary, think about joining a support group or getting help from a therapist.

Overcoming Fear and Panic Attacks

Time Management

To avoid experiencing excessive stress, effectively manage your time and duties. Organise your study or work effectively, set reasonable goals, and use time management strategies to prevent feeling pressed for time or rushed. As an example, if you are a student, study your subjects in a timely manner throughout the year and avoid cramming your studies last minute for exams.

Avoid Avoidance

Refusing to go into some places or circumstances that make you feel anxious shall negatively affect your self-esteem which in turn can make your anxiety worse. With the assistance of a therapist, you can gradually face your discomfort and become less sensitive to anxiety-inducing circumstances.

Relaxation

Make relaxation exercises a part of your everyday routine. You may lessen anticipated worry and maintain your sense of present-moment awareness by using these techniques.

Seek Professional Assistance

It is unfortunate but many who are suffering from anxiety and panic do not seek professional advice because of continued hesitation from an outdated social stigma and a poor understanding of mental ailments. People can be quite sympathetic when an illness is clear and tangible, like a broken arm. Everyone will rush to sign the patients cast and be very supportive. However, when it comes to an affliction affecting the mind, they seem to shrink away due to a lack of knowledge, unfamiliarity, and ignorance.

When facing any ailment, be assertive and if you haven't already, think about scheduling an appointment with a mental health specialist and one that specialises in anxiety and panic disorders, such as a clinical therapist or psychiatrist. For the treatment of panic attacks, evidence-based treatments such as cognitive-behavioural therapy (CBT) and medication have been shown to be successful and will shorten your journey to freedom from panic.

Medication Administration

If you are taking medication for anxiety, take it exactly as recommended and keep your doctor informed of any side effects or concerns on a frequent basis. Never discontinue taking your medicine without first talking to your doctor.

Self-Care

Give yourself permission to prioritise yourself and practice joyful self-care activities. Hobbies, artistic endeavours, reading, time spent in nature, and relaxing and rejuvenating activities are all highly recommended.

Remain Informed

Become more knowledgeable about the mechanics of anxiety and panic attacks. Gaining an understanding of the circumstances that bring them on and their nature will make you feel far less fearful of and much more in control.

Monitor Your Triggers

Maintain a notebook to record the circumstances leading up to your panic episodes as well as your symptoms. This can assist you, or your healthcare team, in identifying trends and creating better plans to control or mitigate triggers.

Overcoming Fear and Panic Attacks

Long-Term Objectives

Make sure your long-term objectives are reasonable. Even if you feel that their development is sluggish. See your future with confidence and take active steps to reach your objectives.

Building a Healthy Life Routine

For sound mental health and wellbeing, developing and upholding healthy routines will have a significant impact on a person's psychological support system and their general quality of life. The structure, consistency, and sense of control that routine offers are essential for promoting mental wellness.

Here we examine the various ways that healthy routines might improve people's psychological and general wellbeing.

Consistency and Foreseeability

Routines provide psychological support; in that they provide consistency and predictability which is very beneficial. Uncertainty and volatility are common in life, and they can cause tension and worry. Establishing routines gives people a daily anchor and a stable structure to help them manage life. A sense of peace and security will be fostered by anticipating and knowing what to expect and when.

Stress and Anxiety Management

People who follow routines are better able to control their stress and anxiety. Setting aside regular times for rest, exercise, and other stress-relieving activities can be made simpler when everyday obligations, chores, and self-care activities are arranged into a clearly defined pattern. Having ingrained stress-reduction techniques in daily routines makes people more resilient to life's obstacles.

Organising Your Time to Be Productive

Effective time management by following well-established routines, which are designed to boost output and give one a sense of achievement. People may maximise their time and resources by prioritising and scheduling their daily duties. People who are more productive tend to feel more in control of their life, which can improve their mental condition and self-esteem.

Regular Self-Care Routines

Self-care practises including consistent exercise, regulating hours of sleep, and a balanced diet are frequently incorporated into routines. These routines are essential for preserving mental and physical well-being. People are more likely to prioritise their well-being when self-care is ingrained in their habit, which lowers the risk of burnout, depression, and other mental health issues.

Control of Emotions

Psychological help frequently include teaching people how to properly control their emotions. Routines can involve techniques that increase an individual's emotional intelligence, such as writing, mindfulness, or meditation. Frequent participation in these activities can enhance emotional regulation, enabling people to handle situations with more resilience and calm.

Let us look at the emotion of anger. Anger is an emotion characterised by a strong sense of antagonism against a person or something that has done you wrong. The great

Overcoming Fear and Panic Attacks

Roman stoic philosopher Lucius Annaeus Seneca said of anger; it is the desire to repay an offence, injury, harm, or injustice. He felt that anger arose in any person that perceived that they had been treated unfairly or that an entitlement, he, or she, had was unjustly taken away. In Seneca's view, it did not matter if such harm was genuine or imagined, just as long as the person believed it to be true.

Seneca also saw anger as a destructive emotion that can arise from within the person's core, and he felt that it can be instigated by either ignorance or arrogance. The first is due to failure to see things according to their true value. The second is where the mind feels that one's dignity has been slighted. He believed, that at times, what people expect, or plan turn out to be different to what actually transpires causes anger, even though this does not mean that a true injustice was done to them.

For example, think of two near-identical scenarios. You are sitting on a table reading a book. Next to you is a couple conversing naturally and happily. In scenario one, you are reading in a café, but in scenario two, you are reading in a public library. You will find that while you are quite calm in scenario one, there is a degree of anger in scenario two.
The reason for this is simply your expectation that there should be silence in a public library. You feel that you have a "right" to everyone's silence and that the couple has taken that "right" away from you.

In short, the next time you feel yourself getting angry about something or someone, stop and think, what entitlement do I feel has been taken away from me? This simple analysis will, in most cases, bring you to the conclusion that the issue is too trivial to induce true anger and you will quickly calm down, saving yourself unnecessary anguish.

Achieving your Goals

Maintaining a regular schedule will help you achieve your long-term objectives. Through the process of deconstructing more ambitious goals into smaller, more doable chores that fit into a daily or weekly schedule, people can advance steadily. This improves confidence and self-efficacy, two important components of psychological well-being, in addition to increasing a sense of accomplishment.

Social Cohesion and Assistance

Socially connected activities and interactions are a common part of routines. These exchanges may serve as an essential source of psychological support. An individual's routine can be greatly enhanced by the presence of friends, family, or support groups, which provide companionship, emotional support, and a feeling of community.

To sum up, healthy habits are essential for boosting emotional health in general, as well as psychological resilience. In a world that is frequently characterised by stress and uncertainty, they provide stability, predictability, and control. Routines build psychological resilience by lowering anxiety, encouraging self-care, enhancing emotional control, and making goal attainment easier. Additionally, routines support people developing strong social ties, which are essential for mental health. Therefore, establishing and preserving healthy habits is an important step in obtaining and preserving the highest level of psychological support and wellbeing.

An excellent illustration of the benefits of routine comes from the armed forces. We are all aware of the obsession army drill sergeants have with a soldier's physical appearance, personal grooming, bed and locker organisation, clothing code, and boot shine. The justification for this comes from

Overcoming Fear and Panic Attacks

the fact that the military discovered long ago that enforcing a rigid schedule gives the troops a degree of control in an environment in which they would otherwise have none. Additionally, such routine enforces antidepressant behaviours on their recruits. Men who are depressed lack drive and tend to pay little attention to their appearance and hygiene, and even stop shaving. They have erratic sleep patterns and are perpetually exhausted. It has proved beneficial to military personnel's psychological stability to force them away from those habits using strict routine.

Sleep Hygiene

The term "sleep hygiene" describes a collection of behaviours and routines that support sound sleep. In addition to being vital for preserving general health, good sleep hygiene may be helpful in averting or treating disorders such as anxiety, stress, and obviously insomnia. To help you achieve a better night's sleep, consider the following important sleep hygiene advice:

Create a Regular Sleep Schedule

Even on weekends, try to stick to the same bedtime and wake-up timings every day. This enhances the quality of your sleep by assisting in the regulation of your body's internal circadian rhythm.

Establish a Calm Night-time Routine

Create a relaxing bedtime ritual to let your body know when it is time to relax. Try reading a book, having a warm bath, using relaxation techniques, or enjoying calming music are some possible activities.

Create a Comfortable Sleeping Environment

Ensure that your bedroom is sleep friendly. This translates into a calm, cool room with comfortable pillows and a mattress. If necessary, take into consideration white noise machines, earplugs, or softer lighting.

Minimise your Screen Time

Your circadian cycle can be upset by the blue light that comes from computers, TVs, phones, and tablets, which can make it difficult for you to go to sleep. Before going to bed, spend at least an hour separated from all such screens.

Control your Night-Time Diet

Stay clear of heavy meals, coffee, and somewhat ironically alcohol, before going to bed. These may cause sleep disturbances or make it more difficult to fall asleep.

Work Out Frequently

Frequent exercise can promote deeper sleep and a quicker rate of sleep onset. But in order to give your body time to calm down, end your workout at least a few hours before going to bed.

Control your Stress

Anxiety and stress can cause sleep disturbances. Before going to bed, control your tension by using relaxation techniques like progressive muscle relaxation, deep breathing, or meditation.

Minimise Naps

While quick power naps are often revitalising, taking prolonged or erratic naps during the day might throw off your sleep schedule. Limit your naps to no more than one or two 15-to-20-minute nap if you must.

Keep your Before Sleep Activities Sedate

When exciting or stressful activities are done close to bedtime, it might be hard to unwind. Before going to bed, try to stay away from demanding conversations, work-related chores, and very self-interesting activities.

Only Sleep and intimacy should be carried out in bed.

Your bed should only be used for sleeping and personal private moments. Avoid using it for anything unrelated to sleeping, such as working or watching TV. This will facilitate and strengthen your brain's association between sleep and the bed.

Minimise Fluid Intake Before Bed

In the evening, consume less of drinks and liquids that encourage diuresis/urination like alcohol, coffee, tea, and soft drinks, a few hours before bedtime. Particularly in men, this should lessen or negate the number of times you have to wake up in the middle of the night to urinate.

Allow Natural Light to Enter Freely into the Area Where You Sleep.

Exposure to daylight, especially in the morning, helps regulate the circadian cycle of your body. It is advisable to partially open your curtains and window blinds after closing your bedroom lights as you go to sleep at night

Register your Thoughts

Consider having a notebook beside your bed to record notions, reservations, or qualms if they are keeping you up at night as racing thoughts or anxieties. You'll be able to relax and clear your head by recording them.

Have Patience

Don't remain in bed kicking and screaming if you couldn't fall asleep in 20 to 30 minutes. When you've tried and failed, get out of bed, engage in a peaceful, non-stimulating activity, and then go back to bed when ready.

It is crucial to understand that developing healthy sleeping patterns may need time, and positive outcomes might not show up right away. When you follow these tips consistently over time, your quality of sleep will improve dramatically. If you're still having trouble falling asleep, you might think about seeing a doctor or sleep expert to rule out any underlying medical illnesses or sleep disorders.

Build Resilience

Developing resilience and engaging in self-care are pivotal for preserving mental and emotional health, particularly when faced with hardship, stress, and obstacles. The capacity to recover from adversity and adjust to change in a constructive way is the very definition of resilience. On the other hand, self-care is giving your physical, mental, and emotional well-being top priority when handling your daily affairs.

Here are some techniques that help you develop resilience and make time for self-care:

Overcoming Fear and Panic Attacks

Cultivate an Optimistic Attitude

Always look ahead and work to develop a cheerful and upbeat outlook. Remind yourself, and focus on, your advantages, your successes, and your capacity for development despite difficult situations. Do not compare yourself to others or dwell on past disappointments or failures. Get up, dust yourself down, and move on.

Enhance Interactions

Keep up and cultivate positive friendships and familial ties. A crucial component of resilience is social support. When necessary, rely on your network of supporters, do not hesitate to use their support to help enhance your emotional wellbeing.

Practise Addressing Problems

Work on acquiring proficient, head-on, problem-solving skills to tackle obstacles. Divide issues into more manageable chunks and look for answers in good time. Do not be too proud to follow the example of others.

Set yourself Sensible Goals

Set long-term, medium-term, and short-term objectives that are attainable. No matter how tiny, acknowledge and celebrate your accomplishments to upturn your self-esteem and drive.

Recognise and accept that life is full of changes. Develop a flexible and adaptive mindset when it comes to how you tackle different circumstances.

Self-Empathy

Treat yourself with love and kindness. Stay away from any

negative self-dialogue or harsh self-criticism. At a minimum, give yourself the same consideration that you give to others.

Develop your Mindfulness

Engage in present-moment awareness and mindfulness. You may enhance your general well-being, manage stress, and lessen anxiety by practising mindfulness and living in the moment (see also page 87).

Create Self-Coping Mechanisms

Handpick healthy coping mechanisms, such as writing, exercise, meditation, or deep breathing, and decide if they are effective for you. Try to handle stresses with these tools.

Panic attacks may be challenging to deal with, especially when making decisions about your educational pursuits and future. You may, however, follow your objectives and effectively negotiate these terrains if you have the appropriate tactics and assistance.

When thinking on your educational or career path after suffering panic attacks, keep the following in mind:

(a) Education-Related Issues

Selecting the Appropriate Course

Choose a course of study that complements your interests and professional objectives while seeking further education. Make sure it complements your tastes and attributes. Make sure that you choose a subject that you are genuinely interested in, and not one that may help satisfy family or loved ones.

Overcoming Fear and Panic Attacks

Modifications

To discuss modifications to accommodate your panic disorder, get in touch with the support services staff at your school or college. They can assist you in getting the support you require, including extra time to take tests or restoration.

Time Handling

Reduce academic stress by developing effective time management and study routines. Avoid leaving course matters to the last minute and then cramming just before exams or deadlines. Make a study plan that also allows and accommodates breaks and time for yourself.

Seek Assistance

Anxiety and panic are quite widespread and common within the student body, and you are not alone. Also, the ailment is only an inappropriate and disorderly engagement of a natural body response. So, if you are experiencing stress or worry related to your academic work, don't be afraid to ask your professors, academic advisers, or counsellors for help. They would have seen this many times before. Also, the better educational establishments provide mental health services particularly to address such issues.

Examine Online or Part-Time Programmes

If attending full-time classes on campus is at this moment too difficult for you, consider online or part-time learning alternatives. These can ease the pressures of a typical academic setting and offer more freedom, until you get a better handle on your condition.

Gradual Advancement

Recognise that moving at your own speed is OK. There's no

need to finish first of your class or ascend too quickly if it is putting too much stress on you. Stress may be better managed with gradual and not steep progress. Make self-care and stress reduction a priority to maintain your general wellbeing as you pursue your educational goals.

(b) Careers-Related Issues

Self-Evaluation

Think carefully about your beliefs, hobbies, and job aspirations. Recognise your true motivations and sources of fulfilment and satisfaction in your daily work. You will be doing this for a long time, and you should at least like what you do.

Sources of Stress

List the specific pressures that you experienced in your previous and present job and how they affected you. You may make more educated judgements regarding your career path if you are aware of your triggers.

Working-Life Harmony

Give work-life balance a priority while selecting or pursuing a career. Look for employment that allows you to have a good work-life balance and is consistent with your ideals.

Positive and Encouraging Workplace

Seek out companies and job settings that understand and cater for mental health issues and help staff members who are experiencing panic or anxiety. An encouraging work atmosphere will have a huge impact.

Overcoming Fear and Panic Attacks

Justifiable Anticipations

In the workplace, set reasonable goals for yourself. Refrain from placing undue pressure on yourself to succeed or prove yourself too rapidly.

Enhancement of Skills

If you want to explore other job alternatives or become more competitive in your chosen sector, think about obtaining new skills or further education e.g., pursuing an MBA.

Seek Adaptable Work Schedules

Look for positions that allow for flexible work schedules or remote work, if at all feasible. This might lessen stressors and provide you greater control over your workspace.

Environmental Factors

Consider stresses due to the environment, such as pollution, noise, or residing in a poorly organised or disorderly area. Discuss such issues with your Health and Safety Directorate.

Never forget how important it is to discuss your demands and difficulties with your employers or teachers. A lot of places of employment and learning have procedures and materials in place to assist people with anxiety or panic disorders. Your education or employment choices should ultimately be in line with your long-term satisfaction and well-being. It is acceptable to modify your plan and look for the assistance you need to accomplish your objectives while controlling panic episodes. Never hesitate to engage career and academic counsellors or seek expert assistance to make well-informed judgements and effectively traverse these domains.

Early Stressor Detection and Treatment

Finding your Stressors

Self-Examination

Give your life and everyday encounters some thought. Keeping a journal can help you keep track of your feelings, ideas, and to pinpoint stressful events.

Physical Indications

Keep an eye out for any physical symptoms of stress, such as palpitations, headaches, stomach problems, tense muscles, tremors, or irregular sleep patterns. These may serve as good indicators of stress.

A shift in emotions

Observe your feelings. Stressors may be indicated by elevated irritability, mood fluctuations, worry, or feelings of frustration or overload.

Daily Life Modifications

Important life events that often cause stress include, having relationship problems, having money troubles, or having health challenges, moving house, starting a new job, etc. Be aware of such events and the stress they carry and prepare for them mentally.

Stressors at Work

Determine the job-related stresses that affect you, such as an overwhelming workload, a lack of control in setting and handling your responsibilities, deadline pressure, office politics, or disagreements and conflicts with co-workers.

Stressors in Relationships

Identify any problems in your personal relationships that are stressing you out, such as issues of sexuality, disagreements with friends, family, or a love partner.
Better communication strategies applied to your various relationships can go a long way in removing many stressors.

Financial Strain

Examine your financial status and try to address any causes of stress related to money, such as restructuring debt, better planning to calculate for unforeseen costs, or addressing the issues of insufficient income.

Medical Factors

Stress can be caused by physical and health conditions, long-term illness, or poor lifestyle decisions (such as eating poorly or not exercising). Be cognisant of such factors and strive to correct what you can.

Appreciate that getting over panic episodes requires patience, determination, and time. On your way to thriving after panic, it is critical to customise these lifestyle changes to suit your requirements and benefit from the individualised advice and support of a healthcare specialist.

CHAPTER 5

LOOKING TOWARD THE FUTURE

Support Network

As humans we are, by our very nature, communal beings. Having a strong support system is crucial for long-term psychological health and may be particularly beneficial for overcoming issues like anxiety or panic attacks. For several crucial reasons, it is very advantageous for an individual experiencing panic attacks to be able to rely on their friends and family for support.

There are many types of support one needs to count on, and these include:

Emotional Support

Talking with loved ones about your experience will help you feel better emotionally when things are hardest. When coping with panic attacks, friends and family may provide understanding, compassion, and a feeling of connection and can be very consoling.

Decreased Sense of Isolation

People who suffer from panic attacks may feel like they are the only ones going through their ordeal, which will make them feel quite isolated. Breaking this loneliness and realising you are not alone in your troubles can be accomplished by simply being able to confide in friends and relatives. As the adage says, "a problem shared, is a problem halved".

Overcoming Fear and Panic Attacks

Validation

Talking with professionals about your condition and getting their understanding will help you feel validated in your experiences. Also knowing that your symptoms, sensations, and reactions are part physical and physiologically grounded—which is the case with panic attacks—will be comforting. Remember, they are an inappropriate body response that can be corrected.

Education

Sharing information with your support group about panic attacks gives you the chance to educate them about the condition. This helps lessen prejudice and misinformation about your condition and allows for the better fostering of both understanding and empathy.

Those who know about your condition might be more sensitive to your welfare and ready to help as and when necessary. They might spot the early warning indicators of a panic attack and provide you with assistance, or aid in handling the situation.

Help with Everyday Duties

When you're experiencing high levels of anxiety, loved ones may provide you with practical support by going with you to therapy sessions or doctor's visits or by volunteering to help with everyday duties reducing your burden while you heal.

Stress Reduction

Hiding your condition from others can represent a difficulty in itself, since you may be further burdened by how to hide your condition, because of your fear that people will judge you if they find out. Talking about your experience helps remove this burden and takes the edge off.

Social Understanding

During social events, friends and relatives who are aware of your condition are more likely to be understanding and accommodating. To make you feel more at ease, they could be open to altering schedules or modifying certain social settings to better suit your healing journey.

Encouragement During Treatment

Your loved one's can help motivate you to stick with your treatment plan and may urge you to seek professional support, such as counselling when needed, and remain resolute in your quest to dominate panic.

It is essential to keep in mind that it is up to you to decide in whom you confide and how much of your experiences to convey. You will need to judge who you trust and who will be understanding or receptive, so you can determine the kind of support you anticipate from different people.

In the end, telling friends and family about your condition can help create a support network that improves your wellbeing and enables you to control and rid yourself of panic attacks. However, when deciding who to choose and how much to reveal about your condition, it is important to consider your personal comfort and wellbeing first.

Identifying Your Trusted Individuals for Your Support Network

First determine who in your life you know you can trust and feel at ease with. This might apply to neighbours, friends, relatives, or co-workers.

When you have selected these individuals, you will need to

Overcoming Fear and Panic Attacks

establish open and honest communication with those chosen for your support network. Talk about your ideas, emotions, and worries—especially if they relate to panic or anxiety episodes that you've had.

In your discussions make sure you accomplish the following:

Educate Them

Keep in mind that they are not experts and not everyone in your chosen support system will have read as much as you have on anxiety and panic attacks. Assist them in comprehending the nature of these ailments, typical triggers, and ways in which they might offer support or comfort.

Establish Limits

Set definite limits with the people in your support system. Inform them openly of your needs for help, including the kind and timing of the same. This helps assure that they can assist in a manner that respects your needs and choices.

Spread Out Your Network

Create an inclusive support system with a variety of connections. While some people might be better at offering practical help or a listening ear, others could be more adept at offering emotional support, etc.

Expert Assistance

Remember you are suffering from a well-defined medical condition, so consider obtaining early assistance from health specialists, such as doctors, counsellors, or therapists, who may provide skilled direction and coping mechanisms. Keep in mind, the earlier you begin to handle the condition the quicker you will dominate it.

Join Support Teams

Seek support groups, either local or virtual, for those suffering from anxiety or panic attacks. Making connections with people who have gone, or are undergoing, similar issues may be quite helpful.

Mutual Assistance

When someone in your network needs assistance, provide it. Creating a mutually beneficial relationship fortifies the connections within your network. Also, the sense that you can help others overcome their difficulties is very empowering.

Frequent Visits

Even when you're not experiencing great difficulties, make time to routinely interact with your support system. By doing this, you keep the connections strong which in turn ensures that you have an effective support network when you need it.

Social Engagement

Engage in social events and get-togethers with the people in your support system. Tightening support connections is the result of spending time together particularly when it is in a fun and comfortable environment.

Clearly Express your Thanks

Openly acknowledge and show gratitude to the people in your support system for their help and patience. Such acknowledgements are the best way of rewarding them for their contributions and strengthens the ties of reciprocity and trust.

Overcoming Fear and Panic Attacks

Handling Conflicts

Deal with disagreements or conflicts within your support system quickly and in a positive and healthy manner. Sustaining solid partnerships requires effective communication and conflict resolution.

Web-Based Communities

Examine internet forums and groups that deal with anxiety and panic attacks. These might offer further resources for information and assistance.

Seek Expert Guidance in Support System Set-up

Consult your therapist or counsellor for guidance when joining or creating a support system that is suited to your unique requirements.

It takes time to create an effective support system, so it is perfectly acceptable to approach people slowly little by little. When it comes to assistance, quality is more important than quantity. A few reliable and willing people who genuinely comprehend your anxieties can provide a strong platform for your mental well-being.

How Best to Articulate About your Condition in an Effective Way

Pick the Appropriate Time and Location

Select a peaceful, tranquil, and cosy space where you may have a private discussion. Select a moment when you, your loved ones, are most at ease and not in a rush.

Get Prepared

Get up-to-date information about your condition before you have the discussion. Be familiar with all the signs, causes, and effects it has on your day-to-day activities. Your explanation will make more sense to your listeners if you are well-rehearsed and well-informed.

Communicate Your Emotions Openly

Begin by being open and honest about your feelings and emotions. Explain the physical and mental symptoms that anxiety and panic attacks cause you. When describing your experiences, stay personal and use "I" phrases. For example, "I often feel overwhelmed when..."

Explain Your Prognosis

Inform your loved ones of the medical diagnosis that you have received from a medical practitioner. Clarity and validation of your experiences will come from having a definite diagnosis.

Have Empathy and Patience

Recognise that your loved ones can be unsure or worried about how to deal with what you are telling them. When responding to their reactions, use empathy and patience. It is acceptable if they require some time to assimilate and understand the information you are providing.

Simplify Your Language

Try as best you can to steer clear of technical or medical terminology. Make sure your loved ones get what you're going through using language that is plain and

Overcoming Fear and Panic Attacks

uncomplicated.

Talk About your Needs

Make sure your loved ones and friends know exactly what you need from them. When you communicate your needs, they are more able to provide you with the emotional support, understanding, or the targeted actions you require.

Promote Inquiries

If your loved ones have any questions, encourage them to inquire. Respond to their inquiries in an open and sincere manner. This inspires greater comprehension. Talk about any coping mechanisms or treatments you have used or intend to employ. Therapy, medicine, self-help methods, and lifestyle modifications are a few examples of this.

Provide Assurance

Make it clear to your loved ones that you're grateful for their support and that you're taking proactive action to control your condition. Discuss with your loved ones how to respect boundaries. For instance, inform them if you need time alone when having a panic attack.

Subsequent Actions

Keep checking in with your loved ones after the discussion. Do provide them with updates on your health and any changes that have occurred.

Since discussing your condition with family and friends is an important step to take, it would be advisable to first discuss it with your therapist or counsellor. They can help you get ready for the discussion and offer direction on how to handle any barriers that may arise. In the end, having open and honest conversations with your loved ones will end up resulting in useful empathy and support while you manage your condition.

Never forget that following your dreams and interests is an individual and distinctive path. It is alright to take your time and modify when necessary to suit your personal situation.
If you observe self-care, build support, and maintain persistence, you will achieve your goals and experience the pleasure that comes with it.

Overcoming Fear and Panic Attacks

In Conclusion

I hope that this book will help you navigate the maze of panic disorder. Note that you have been battling panic unarmed and defenceless. This has now changed.

Recognise that panic is an exaggerated and inappropriate body response and nothing else. Do not feel embarrassed or lessoned by it. Your ability to face your panic episodes head-on and your strength and resilience are what define you in the end, not the panic attacks you currently suffer from. As you proceed on your path to recovery and healing, bear in mind these fundamental concepts always:

The first step in treating panic disorder is understanding it. Knowledge is true power. Apply the new mindset in how you face panic. You can take charge using the knowledge and techniques you have acquired from this book.

Despite the feeling of isolation that sometimes accompany panic disorder, you are not the only person going through this and there are many, many fellow suffers out there. Don't be afraid to ask your family, friends, or support networks for assistance. Talking about your experiences with others can be very healing.

The road to recovery may not always be smooth; there will be ups and downs. When working to conquer panic disorder, have patience with yourself and endure. Know that even the smallest victories represent progress.

Making self-care a priority is crucial for controlling panic disorder. Your entire well-being may be greatly improved by adopting stress-reduction strategies, healthy lifestyle choices, and consistent routines.

Medical experts, therapists, and counsellors are important partners in your rehabilitation process. Seek their input and help early. Ignore any social stigma you may carry and deal with things as you would for many other medical or surgical condition. Acceptance and mindfulness are effective strategies for controlling panic. Panic attack anxiety can be significantly reduced by practising mindfulness and embracing your emotions without passing judgement.

Treatment for panic attacks frequently entails combining a variety of techniques and approaches, many of which are described in this book. In my opinion, changing your mindset on how to react and address your panic is essential. Additionally, medication (like antidepressants or anxiety medications), treatments (like cognitive-behavioural therapy), and lifestyle changes can also be used to assist people in managing and reducing the frequency and intensity of panic episodes.

Finally, keep in mind that you are more than strong enough to conquer panic disorder, it is just in the way you apply that strength. I trust that this book's pages have given you information, resources, and confidence that will help you achieve your task.

May you discover resilience, serenity, and a life full of happy and peaceful moments as you travel forward on your journey. This is only one episode in your life, but one that you will now be drafting on your own terms—one of personal development, bravery, and success.

Overcoming Fear and Panic Attacks

NOTE SECTION
Write any notes in the empty pages set out below

Dr. Mashal Al Nawab

Notes

ABOUT THE AUTHOR

Dr. Mashal Al Nawab
MBChB, DipRCPath, MRCPath, CCST, FRCPath, PhD (Lond)

The author is a Consultant Pathologist and Medical Researcher and has practiced Clinical Pathology at a Senior level in both England and the Middle East. He is a fellow of the Royal College of Pathologists in the United Kingdom and has a doctorate in Pathology from the University of London.

He has authored several peer reviewed medical papers in pathology and was previously an Honorary Senior Lecturer in Pathology in the University of London. He is a winner of the Presidents Prize of the Royal Society of Medicine of the United Kingdom and Northern Ireland.

He maintains a special interest in examining the complexities and remedies surrounding anxiety and depression, particularly in relation to ageing, alongside other age-related challenges. Additionally, he is dedicated to formulating protocols aimed at improving the quality of life of the elderly.

Printed in Great Britain
by Amazon